# ABD-RU-SHIN
# QUESTIONS AND ANSWERS

ABD-RU-SHIN

# QUESTIONS
# AND
# ANSWERS

1924–1937

ALEXANDER BERNHARDT PUBLISHING CO.
VOMPERBERG · TYROL

This book "Questions and Answers" by Abd-ru-shin contains the translation according to the sense of the original German text. In the translation the expressions and sentences used by Abd-ru-shin to mediate the Living Word to the human spirit can only be rendered approximately.

The reader should therefore realise that this translation cannot replace the original. However, if he makes the effort – as is desired by the Author – to absorb the contents intuitively, he will recognise the significance of this work for mankind, despite the deficiencies arising out of a translation.

I often receive letters of genuine gratitude, which arouse great joy in me. The serious seeker, however, who through the lectures has become a finding one, can express his thanks for that only to God Himself. Although I have been able to become the mediator, the *gift* is not from me. I am nothing without God, and could give nothing without Him.

As an example I would only like to cite the following: When a gift is brought to a man by a servant, he does not thank the servant, but the giver himself. It is no different here. If I am permitted to draw from sources which are closed to others, then surely I myself have the greatest cause for thanking Him Who grants me this!

# 1

QUESTION:

*The lecture on "Fate" raises the question of how justice takes effect in the reciprocal action on people who make large donations, not with their intuitive perception, but by practising charity merely because it is the "fashion", or in order to make a "name" for themselves.*

ANSWER:

The process can be clearly surveyed. It takes place exactly according to the Laws. The environment of every human being is permeated by the nature of his *actual* intuitive perception, and thus forms a homogeneous ethereal layer around him. Self-deceptions are automatically excluded from these processes, as they are not viable. Now if a person has cultivated within himself an honest, good volition, then also the layer surrounding him will be of a like nature. Returning reciprocal actions of an evil nature, dating from former times, are now held up by this layer opposing them, and are diverted, or absorbed and disintegrated, before they are able to strike the person himself, and are thus either completely eliminated or at least considerably weakened, so that through his earnest good volition he has thereby received forgiveness for the former evil.

It is the reverse with those who actually do good through donations, but only with the intention of gaining something for themselves, whether it is merely to become well-known, thus out of vanity, or to receive some rank or title, thus out of ambition.

The Law of Reciprocal Action will be fulfilled absolutely, in every respect. From that point where his gift has brought about blessing, the good will flow back to the donor in any case, of the same nature as the good that it has brought about. In this instance however the inner being, and accordingly also the environment of the donor, are permeated with egotism, the urge for personal advantage, or some other evil. The good now streaming back will first strike this layer, and will likewise be held up by it, diverted, absorbed and disintegrated, so that the person himself can receive nothing of this good reciprocal effect, or at best only a very weakened part of it.

Whether the returning flow of good is entirely diverted, or to what extent it is weakened before reaching the person inwardly and thereby actually becoming effective, depends solely on the strength of the intuitive perception of the one concerned. If this is strongly evil, it is his own fault if the good ordained for him in the reciprocal effect cannot reach him. But if the evil is less strong, a part of the good will penetrate to him after all, whereby he will then receive exactly according to his actual inner value, no more and no less. It comes close to him, and in this way can take effect quite well in his environment, in outer earthly things, which are transient; but it cannot touch him personally so that he could have eternal gain from it, which alone is of value.

Here is already a distinction: If the person concerned gives out of an open intuitive perception, solely for the sake of helping, then a thread is immediately formed which, emanating from him, reaches that point where through his help the blessing springs forth, and forms the direct path back to him for the reciprocal action.

Through this the effect is a much more direct, more concentrated one. However, if his intuitive perception does not participate in the same way when giving, then this thread emanating from him, as the connection with the place where his gift takes effect, is missing; because it has led to what is homogeneous with the intuitive perception. Hence the good reciprocal action cannot reach him in such a concentrated form either.

In addition, many other secondary circumstances are also involved, mention of which could only confuse the picture, although they all contribute to give the most delicate shadings to the nature of the justice which takes effect in the reciprocal action, so that one simply cannot imagine even an atom of injustice in all that takes place. This possibility is completely ruled out through the wonderful interworking of the wise Laws of the Creator, so that everyone receives what is due to him, most accurately weighed. However, it must be remembered here that seldom does much of all this take place during one short earth-life, but only fragments. The entire happening is spread over man's whole existence.

# 2

QUESTION:

*Is a judge spiritually absolved from responsibility if through ambition he becomes over-zealous in his service, putting aside what is generally understood by humaneness in the conviction that thereby he is fulfilling his duty?*

ANSWER:

For such a person it would be better never to have been born. The protective wall of "service and duty" is withdrawn at earthly death. He is *absolutely personally* responsible for all his decisions and actions, as is every other human being. An earthly wrongly-adjusted conviction alters nothing of it. This can only deceive him personally. It always depends upon *how* he performs his office. He must take love as the basis; for only in true love does justice lie.

# 3

QUESTION:

*(a) What about preachers who regard their office only as a means of earning a living, and do not really believe in all they teach? (b) Does a Communion administered by such persons really have any effective power?*

ANSWER:

(a) Reciprocal effects take no heed of earthly positions and dignities, but give to each person what he deserves. Therewith *all* such questions are solved. (b) The effect of the Communion depends mainly upon the inner life *of the recipient*. If he is rightly attuned to it, he will receive the power in accordance with his attunement, even though the Communion be administered by such a hand. When Christ specially emphasised in all things: "As thou hast believed, so shall it be done unto thee!", He always clearly refers to the Law of Reciprocal Action. Each one can receive only that to which he is attuned, nothing else. Whether it be spiritual or physical powers. Otherwise it would be easy for injustice to flow into the Holy Laws of Creation. And that is impossible.

# 4

*Abd-ru-shin says that not all human beings are chil-
dren of God. But it is written: He who denies the
adoption by God sins against the Holy Spirit!*

ANSWER:

What is written also requires first of all to be rightly
understood. Thanks therefore to the enquirer for asking
this question. Those who ask in this way often give
something to many people thereby, without being aware
of it.

The lecture "Man and his free will", in which it is
stated that not all human beings are children of God, at
the same time also answers the question asked above.
The adoption by God is not denied by the fact that not
all men are children of God.

The adoption by God is only denied by that person
who neglects the abilities for the adoption by God which
are contained in his spirit-seed-grain, that is to say,
which were given to him by the Holy Spirit, thus
developing them insufficiently and allowing them to
become stunted, so that they cannot come to value and
to growth. *That is the denial of the adoption by God!* In
this negligence lies a denial. Thus it goes without saying
that at the same time he also sins against the Holy Spirit,
Who gave to him in the seed-grain the abilities for the
adoption by God, so that they should be developed and
cultivated.

Whoever fails to do this will never be or become a

child of God despite his expectation of it, that is to say the possibility of it, which the gift of the Holy Spirit had promised him even in the seed-grain. Through disregarding, thus denying this gift, he has sinned, and thereby made impossible the fulfilment of the high promise.

# 5

QUESTION:

*What effect and what spiritual purpose has confirmation in the Protestant church?*

ANSWER:

Confirmation would have a spiritual effect and a spiritual purpose, and could without doubt even bring great blessing, if it had as its basis a pure spiritual significance. As it is, however, this is *not* the case; on the contrary, confirmation is not in the least concerned with religion or faith as such – something that should be the essence of *every* act consummated before the Altar, that is before the Table of the Lord; rather is confirmation merely an act of the church as an organisation, which thereby puts it on the same level as some practice of an organisation.

The proof that this is so, and cannot be otherwise, lies in the fact that neither psychic value, inner maturity, longing for the Godhead, nor even spiritual knowledge is decisive for admission to confirmation by the Protestant church. For the church just flatly rejects any such examination unless the "rule of its organisation" is complied with; which without exception systematically stipulates that a confirmation may be performed *only if* the applicant has attended confirmation classes for a specified number of months, under a minister appointed by the church for the purpose, that is under an official of the church.

Thus it is not possible to be confirmed, even if the

applicant declares his willingness to undergo any examination regarding soul and spirit, by which he may demonstrate his worthiness and maturity for confirmation. Consequently, even mature and valuable human beings are not admitted to confirmation by the church, and are rejected on account of this regulation, if they have acquired their maturity and worth not through an official of the church but in some other way, although this may very often be much more valuable than the intellectual confirmation classes.

It is self-evident that in no circumstances may these regulations be applied if it is a question of a person's spiritual and psychic gain. Such a thing would be hindering and working directly against the Sublime Will of Christ, in which the church as such *must* be active. By no means would it be in the spirit and according to the wishes of the great Saviour, Who never intended to found a church or a religion, but Whose Mission it was to set the souls *free*.

For this reason confirmation *must* be only a pure formality, merely an admission to the *organisation* of the church as such. It must not be mistaken for a closer relationship with God. Therefore it can likewise bring only organisational benefits and organisational obligations to the people who are confirmed, nothing else.

The church itself will probably also regard it in this light, because otherwise it would be guilty through exclusion of a negligence and a presumption which would be bound to have a very serious reciprocal effect. Quite apart from the fact that it would be equivalent to a dangerous conceit, which was hardly greater among the Pharisees at the time of Christ. *And that is not to be expected of the church!* For since the Christian churches work only in the spirit of Christ, and according to His teaching, such a restrictive regulation proves that confirmation does *not* pertain to spiritual acts or to matters which bring advancement, but can only be a formality of the worldly organisation.

Were it otherwise, the restriction through the regulations would indicate an error, the significance of which needs no elucidation. Thus confirmation cannot really be considered as a part of spiritual ascent. What the individual gains inwardly through this act comes through his own, his personal attitude.

# 6

*It is repeatedly pointed out in modern books that one day will come the time of the God-men, the perfect noble human beings. Is that the time of the Millennium?*

ANSWER:

It is not the time of the God-*men* that will come, but the time of the God-*man!* Here again the mistake lies in the attempt to generalise a *personal* promise, which hitherto has not been understood.

There can never be God-men other than the One Who issued from God: Imanuel, the Son of Man. The most perfect, noble human beings, in their highest perfection, can in the nature of things become only *spirit*-men, but never Divine.

# 7

QUESTION:

*Has the Grail Movement any connection with one of the existing Grail Orders, or with any such societies with similar names?*

ANSWER:

The Grail Movement has *no* connection *whatever* with any of the known orders or societies. In its absolute independence it would also reject any connection.

# 8

*Will not Abd-ru-shin also comment on many a burning social and political question?*

ANSWER:

I will *not* comment on social politics and the like! While thousands of others may do so freely and unmolested, with me people would undoubtedly look for an ulterior motive in it; for strange to say they always try to impute, even to my harmless endeavours and purely objective and logical lectures, intentions that are far from my mind. I would even like to withdraw from the *most private* conversations, to which any other person has an *unconditional right*. Out of these the most repulsive antagonism has often arisen for me. If in answer to a question I merely give an *allegory*, or for illustrative purposes make use of things that have been seen, for instance from serious research circles of well-known mediums, with particular reference to them ... someone will quickly be found to distort it and try to impute it to me *personally*, and will swiftly spread it abroad with embellishments and additions of his own fantasy, or even exploit it for shady purposes.

What is the use, when in the eyes of serious men such incidents merely throw the limelight on *those* who try to harm me thereby? What is the use, when thereupon assurances always come to me from many quarters that this is the best proof of *how seriously my words are taken!* The abhorrence remains with me all the same. If this is so even in the spiritual field, what would it be like in other fields!

Therefore I prefer to be silent, although with the same simplicity and certainty I could also clearly throw light on so many things, and indicate many a path. I wish to continue and complete my work, which meets with so much approval, in peace. For this reason I request that in future questions of this nature be no longer sent.

# 9

QUESTION:

*Will Abd-ru-shin also bring enlightenment on the art of breathing?*

ANSWER:

At some future time I shall also speak about the art of breathing. The well-known teachings about it are good, and indeed thousands will have already experienced their blessings on themselves. My lecture about it, however, is to bring *greater* enlightenment. It will only further, and not reject, what already exists on the subject; and will indicate *new* paths, and make it possible for all those who occupy themselves with or seek it to become fully aware of the *real* processes, which today are not yet known at all; and through which they will advance all the more easily, quickly, and further than hitherto.

# 10

*Is church attendance advisable for seekers?*

ANSWER:

The way to the Truth goes also through the churches. The decisive factor for it is always and only the inner state of the individual. Through attending church a man will advance if it really serves to compose him, to incite him to turn his inner self away from all earthly trivialities during that time, and to seek connection with the Light. Many people *need* to attend church. According to how *he*, the individual, opens himself, so much will he receive. Some people find devoutness only in the woods, others on the seashore, others again in music, and many people actually *only* in church. The latter should *not* stay away from churches!

In *all* denominations there are preachers who deserve to be described as born to it, that is, called to it. Man must simply learn to become inwardly *alive*, to weigh and examine what is offered to him; for he is indeed solely responsible for himself. As soon as he makes the effort he will already sense precisely what is right.

Naturally church-going alone cannot bring a person any blessing; it avails him nothing unless he himself *awakens* inwardly to it!

It rests with each one himself, and ever again only with him, whether inwardly he moves upwards, or towards the Darkness. Rightly considered, even wandering for short distances on wrong paths can also only benefit him; for he will recognise how he should *not* act, and will guard against it in future. He must always use the fragments of such a path as steps, which will lead him upwards all the more quickly. The churches are quite good, but the people, *those who attend* these churches, are inwardly dead. If they bring life into themselves, they will also find what they need in the *churches*.

# 11

QUESTION:

*What happens if after the granting of a prayer a person falls back again into his old faults?*

ANSWER:

Alas, in most cases man only succeeds in praying to his God with utter fervour when in dire need. Once the need has passed, his prayers quickly become more superficial, more trivial; and often with the fulfilment all the intentions of the one who at first implored so urgently cease, because "other, more necessary interests" confront him. Everything again becomes matter-of-course, commonplace, inferior. The thoughts are differently focussed, on superficial, earthly matters.

But this is a well-known process, which even thousands of years ago was no different from today.

Illness, for instance, gives man time for reflection, which later he imagines he no longer has, simply because he again allows himself to be too much diverted from it, sometimes by rather trivial matters. Never will he be honest enough to admit that he simply does not want it otherwise!

Just let us keep to the sick. Some sick person knows that the end must come, however long it may yet take. It is obvious that under perhaps tormenting pain his thoughts will become more serious, in view of the end of that illness and thus of his departure. Also that thereby he becomes psychically softened and mellow. Probably there also awaken in him all kinds of thoughts and good intentions of how altogether differently he would adjust his life if, against all expectations, he could once more be freed from the pain, and ... need not die yet. Quite timorously, as an unlikely, great, unmerited fortune, such a possibility lights up in the far distance.

But thoughts of this nature reflect hidden wishes, and are often more heartfelt prayers than the direct supplication for recovery, because in such situations they are really pure and humble.

If, to the surprise of many, the grace of unexpected improvement is bestowed on such a person, it often happens that with the gradual strengthening of the sick body the former faults also arise once more! And then comes what has so often happened already, and will often happen still: The man indeed believes of himself that he is proceeding on the new paths which he has resolved to take, but in reality they are the *old paths* once more, only in a new form. Thus the power of the free will becomes a curse instead of a blessing.

With every fresh downward sliding the horizon of his understanding naturally also narrows, so that he can never perceive this sliding down, and does not believe others who seek to draw his attention to it in time; and suddenly he is more heavily burdened with guilt than before. These are the kind of cases where it would have been better if help had never come. Therefore the granting of a petition does not bring absolute blessing to every human being.

For such a person, however, who can be said to have broken his word, no flash of lightning will now come from On High to punish him, nor will he immediately fall ill again and die. Only naïve and ignorant minds expect such things. This would indeed be an arbitrary act of the Creator, contrary to His own Laws. If in His Mercy He has granted recovery or improvement, this help has come about in the natural course of events, entirely within the framework of the perfect Laws. Nothing else. The Creator cannot and will not simply take away this recovery or improvement, just because the help was bestowed as a gift upon a human being who later, through his free will and his old faults, has become unworthy. Renewed illness will then only ensue through a fresh physical cause, unless a remnant of the old illness was still left, which once more comes into renewed activity.

It would therefore be wrong to see perhaps an injustice of the Creator in cases occurring in this way, or even to think that the improvement would have come in any case, and was no special act of Grace at all. But it is worse still to live under the delusion that the continued well-being proves that this human being is holding to the right path!

This last contains the greatest of dangers! A self-deception so beautiful, so comforting, that many people gladly delude themselves with it. Man's guilt in this may not be perceived for years, perhaps not even until he has to pass on. Then, however, he will very quickly recognise what he has done. They are people to be pitied, not always condemned.

But as here with illness, so is it also with the granting of other prayers, as in general with *every* gift from On High! Also when a man, already from birth or only at a certain time, has received a special talent for some purpose which he does not fulfil aright, the talent is not then immediately taken from him. But it cannot achieve *that* upswing which it would otherwise have attained on the *right* path.

In any case, it is very considerably obscured and spoiled with regard to *that* purpose for which it was actually given. However, this incapacity does not at the same time extinguish the longing still to work towards the high goal. If in addition there is a narrowing of the ability to comprehend, the result is a mixture which causes much harm and confusion. Such a person unquestioningly believes that he stands completely in the fulfilment of his task, and is also proceeding on the right path, likewise that he is achieving something in it. And yet everything is wrong.

The person so blessed with grace, who is not fulfilling, lacks every help from the Light, to Which he has closed himself, and thus he also lacks the necessary guidance. Pretending to know it himself, and better, is of no avail to him. For him it becomes the worst snare of his life. As soon as he then passes over, he must render account for all the gifts entrusted to him, as Christ in so many parables strikingly illustrates the process of the release of the unconditional reciprocal action. –

The foregoing explanations are only to serve the questioner as an approximate guideline for his own observations, which according to his question he surely wishes to make. But everything he wants to know is already clearly stated in my lectures, he need only follow aright every course of the happening.

# 12

QUESTION:

*The publisher's sign on the books and other publications is a puzzle to many readers, and arouses the desire to learn its meaning. Ignorant or ill-disposed people have even sought to find a rather strange explanation indeed for it, wishing to represent the snake as evidence that ' with his lectures Abd-ru-shin unconsciously works for the Darkness, and therefore for what is wicked and evil. The snake here being regarded as the symbol of all evil.*

ANSWER:

Well, such can surely be offered only to completely ignorant and thoughtless people. Those with any degree of education will know that the snake biting its tail also symbolises something entirely different and the very opposite, as for example the concept of infinity. Thus the A and the circle of the snake could very well mean that my studies seek to fathom infinity, or that my lectures deal with what takes place in infinity. It can just as well be said, however, that the snake is not intended to portray the concept of infinity, but the O, and therefore what the publisher's sign indicates is: The publisher endeavours to convey all that can be the A and the O of spiritual knowledge, thus which lies between the beginning and the end. And *that* is really what the sign is meant to indicate.

# 13

QUESTION:

*Why does Abd-ru-shin have so many opponents?*

ANSWER:

I have hostility, but no opponents. These are two different things. Only one who knows how to reply to something in a purely objective way can be considered an honest opponent, since I too always and only remain purely objective and impersonal. But such people as show hostility to me personally are not worthy to be called opponents. In and by their hostility they always give evidence of their great inner poverty, and at the same time prove by their manner that indeed they must possess really despicable qualities; for otherwise they would not do such things. Opposition is something quite different, much more honest, and never anything personal.

# 14

QUESTION:

*From what group has Abd-ru-shin emerged, and what training has he had? How did he acquire what he states in his lectures?*

ANSWER:

These questions have whizzed towards me after lectures. I will reply to them again here with equal brevity:

I have not emerged from any group, nor have I had any training, I have not studied or acquired the knowledge from anywhere. I have not hitherto read any Buddhist, theosophical or anthroposophical work, nor any other, but reject all such books as soon as they are offered to me. Or else I take them, but do not read them.

What I state in my lectures I speak with conviction from out of myself. And if similarities are to be found in various religions, I certainly have not derived them from these. I am glad, however, when the same or similar things are noted in them.

For all these reasons I always demand that a person should examine the words, but pay no heed to the speaker! Whoever *then* wishes to follow me is a really serious seeker, one who knows how to think for himself. And others, who have to concentrate on persons instead of on the subject, and consequently cannot remain objective, have no value for a serious onward-striving. For me even less as a human being.

# 15

QUESTION:

*Recently I read the following in a newspaper article: "The piercing of the body of Christ, and the raising of it on the cross, was the world-historical event of the reconciliation of the Godhead with mankind; it was the most important happening in all history, to which all deeper religious thought, before Christ and after Christ, is more or less related."*

*Shortly before this I had read the very enlightening lecture by Abd-ru-shin about the death on the cross of the Son of God. Could not an answer along the lines of this lecture be given in the same paper? Surely many people would be deeply interested.*

ANSWER:

If this view is to represent the depth of religious thought, it is in a bad way. I shall not participate in a daily paper.

Quite apart from the fact that in any case the paper would refuse publication of a contradictory article, which I could not bring myself to ask for because I myself take my lectures far too seriously, I simply would not have time for it even with the best intention. But also reverence for the subject itself forbids me to enter into an exchange of public opinions in daily newspapers.

Any really serious seeker will not be content either with such articles and explanations, and in the end will surely find his way to my lectures, and then like yourself recognise with dismay the inaccuracy of many of the views hitherto held. As you have already read the lecture, it is unnecessary for me to enter more fully into the subject itself.

Moreover, anyone who is only to some extent capable of thinking impartially must find a serious flaw in the view expressed in the article, which will not leave him in peace, and will urge him all the more to look seriously for the Truth. Surely any person who is inwardly alive would find it very difficult to accept that, of all things, a crime and murder committed on the Messenger Who issued from the Divine should bring about the reconciliation of this Godhead with mankind!

God allowed His Son to come from all Glory on to this gloomy earth, among men who had turned away from Him, in order to show them the way upwards to His Luminous Kingdom through the explanations in His Word, which may also be called Message or Teaching.

That this mankind, for whom the Message of God was intended, then rejected the Messenger, persecuted Him with hatred and finally even tortured and murdered Him, was a consequence of their sin or their wrongdoing in having raised the earthly intellect to be their actual ruler in place of God. But instead of later acknowledging this new guilt to be the fruit of the great Fall of Man, they ultimately even exalted this murder and rejection of God's Messenger to an all-glorifying Festival of Reconciliation between the thus criminal mankind and the Godhead Whom they had outraged through this murder. Really going rather far. How does this strange mankind picture their Godhead, that they imagine they can treat Him in such a way with impunity?

# 16

QUESTION:

*It is often said: "The Lamb of God, that beareth the sins of the world!" But Abd-ru-shin's lecture "The Crucifixion of the Son of God and the Last Supper" explains in a way which I can understand that, in accordance with the immutable Laws of the Creator, Christ could not take upon Himself the burden of the sins of the world. How then does Abd-ru-shin explain this contradiction?*

ANSWER:

In the *Word* Itself lies no contradiction. This lies solely in the hitherto false interpretation. "Behold the Lamb of God, that beareth the sins of the world" does not at all mean that It has taken upon Itself the sins of the world and the guilt of men, and so has taken them from the world and from men, as indolent humanity in their well-known boundless arrogance would like to have it; but rather: In His wound-marks Christ visibly bears the sin of the world, its crime, which was perpetrated against Him as the Messenger of God.

The Lamb bears the marks of the world's sin as a perpetual accusation! By no means as a token of reconciliation.

In the visions of John, too, the accusation is repeated more than once, quite specifically: "The Lamb that was slaughtered!" This expression, the frequent outcry of the Elders before the Throne of God during the *Judgment*, does not sound in the least like rejoicing over reconciliation, but like an accusation, and clearly indicates the crime which was thereby committed.

Therefore it would be much better if humanity were to take the increasing number of stigmatisations (appearance of the wound-marks on mediumistic persons) as serious warnings, rather than to rejoice about them.

All this is surely somewhat more intelligible and clear than the peculiar interpretation to the contrary, which simply wants to burden the pure Divine with the sins of mankind. Now there is apparently only a slight outward difference as such in this new version, and yet it is the opposite of what has hitherto prevailed, but absolutely the right one if the perfection of the Divine Laws from the beginning is not to be held in doubt, that is if the Perfection of God Itself, Which cannot permit of any deviation in justice either towards others or towards Itself, is acknowledged and thereby considered!

Also when it is written in the Revelation of John, Chapter VII, verses 14 and 15: "These are they which came out of great tribulation, and have washed their robes, and made them white in the blood of the Lamb. Therefore are they before the throne of God, and serve him day and night in his temple; and he that sitteth on the throne shall dwell above them", all this is only an absolute confirmation of my lectures.

Think of my numerous references and explanations about the ethereal body in the beyond, which is called garment, robe of the spirit, or covering. Those human beings who absorbed Christ's Word, and *lived* according to It, subsequently and quite naturally made their ethereal body, their garment, literally less dense and dark, hence purer, lighter and brighter, so that thereby they were able to float upwards until they finally reached the Luminous Kingdom of God, also called Paradise, above which, outside the Primordial Creation, the Divine dwells or has Its being. Thus they are *those* human spirits who have lived according to the Word of Christ, and thereby followed the way which He pointed out to them.

This being-washed-clean in the blood also means nothing else; for Christ, like all genuine Messengers of the Lord, was not received joyfully by mankind, but as an enemy of the intellectual domination He was scorned, scourged, tortured and finally even put to death by its adherents. He had to shed His blood because those who at that time wished to lead spiritually did not like the Message He brought, since they too had submitted to the intellect and therefore could not "understand" a Message from God.

Thus he who absorbed in a living way His Word, on account of Which He was condemned as a blasphemer, thereby figuratively washed himself with His blood. For the Word made it possible for him to walk on the right path, which alone was capable of washing him clean, and which through the violent death of the Bringer of the Word is marked with His blood. This, however, signifies no reconciliation of God with humanity, and alters nothing of the crime of the crucifixion. Nor does it speak for a burdening with or assuming of the guilt of men.

Just reflect quietly once more yourself, upon what is stated, clear and distinct: "...have washed their robes and made them white!" Just read this aright! Therewith it is explicitly stated: *They have done it themselves!* It is not Christ Who has washed their robes for them. Therefore He did not take their guilt upon Himself, but they themselves had to wash off their sins! Thus the reverse of the opinion held by so many spiritually empty believers.

Also the further statements in the Revelation of John, describing the fate of mankind, clearly enough express the opposite, when the vials of the *Wrath* of God are poured out over the earth and mankind; which surely cannot be interpreted as a sign and expression of reconciliation through the blood of Christ violently shed by men, but clearly enough as a punishment!

Whoever refuses to understand aright what is everywhere clearly expressed, and what is also quite obvious to all logical thinking, can naturally not be helped. Such people are too indolent to pull themselves together and must perish therein, because without purifying their garments for themselves they cannot ascend to the Light. There are so many searching in the Bible, and they all read wrongly even today. These will always remain Bible-searchers, and never become Bible-knowers.

My lectures so far have already given sufficient information about everything. If man allows these to become alive within him, the bandage will thereby also fall from his eyes, and they will at last, without my help, see everything clearly in the Light of Truth which hitherto has still been somewhat strange to them. Right up to the highest luminous part of Creation, they will no longer find any gaps in all the happenings therein from the Primordial beginning until today, and they will even recognise what *must* ensue from them for the future. Without any mysticism and secrecy, and without laborious, unreliable calculation.

# 17

QUESTION:

*Is it asking too much if I request Abd-ru-shin to explain his attitude in regard to the sublime thought of the Buddhists, which finds its greatest bliss in the dissolution of the human spirit that has attained to perfection?*

ANSWER:

Your question at the same time contains the answer within it. Indeed I most decidedly set myself *against* this thought, I *oppose* it in the *strictest* sense of the word! The highest bliss of the perfected human spirit is the *personally conscious life* in the spiritual part of Creation which is called Paradise, as well as the personally conscious co-operation from thence in the continual development of Creation according to the Divine Will. If dissolution had to take place, all human existence, the journeying through all the parts of Creation, would be utterly pointless! But this again cannot be reconciled with the Perfection of the Creator's Will.

Eventually, everyone will also find that the dissolution of a complete human spirit can never be progress, but only a dreadful retrogression! Even in Paradise the human spirit will perpetually develop further in its abilities, but it will never become dissolved, because the final goal of its journeying, and of all the necessities for development associated with it, is to become self-conscious, developing into the personal "ego".

Dissolution strikes only *that* human spirit which goes astray on its course through the material because of wrong views, thus losing the right way and not finding the way back to that Luminous Height whence it originates. Then when the part of the world which it inhabits drives on towards its disintegration, the spirit with its material coverings is likewise quite naturally disintegrated and dissolved, whereby it also loses its ego as such, which had become personal. It thereby ceases to exist as a personality. This dissolution is the same as being effaced for ever from the Golden Book of Conscious Life, because the spirit was useless and did not seek its way to the height.

The process is a quite natural, automatic happening, called eternal damnation. The most dreadful thing that can happen to a human spirit which has become personally conscious.

But a spirit which develops towards the height takes on more and more the image of the Creator, and in a human ideal form it enters the Spiritual Realm personally conscious of itself, so that there it may continually increase its co-operation in the work of Creation. To go still higher is impossible for it, nor can this ever be brought about through a dissolution, which simply cannot take place in an upward direction; for then the spirit's path would have to lead beyond the boundary of Creation, and that it cannot do. Above this then comes the Divine. The human spirit, however, is of spiritual and not Divine origin; and this immutably defines the exact, natural and insurmountable boundary for it. It must remain in the Spiritual Realm because of its origin, which cannot undergo any change in itself, nor any intensification towards the Divine. Consequently the Buddhist thought, which moreover is also cultivated by many occultists in the belief that they bear Divinity within them, is definitely an error. Man is a creature, thus he stands *in* Creation, and will always have to remain *in* it. Any other assertion merely shows a ridiculous presumption, from which indeed all mankind suffer so much, and thereby consider the most fantastic and unnatural things to be possible.

The Buddhist thought of a supreme bliss through dissolution of the laboriously-gained personal ego-consciousness has its origin in the propensity of the Orientals for comfortable contemplation! This propensity has also crept as a wish into the religious views, which always bear some characteristic stamp of the country in which they arose.

# 18

*Abd-ru-shin declares that not every human being is a child of God; but it is written that every human being bears within him as a heritage the adoption by God, and thus has a claim to the Kingdom of God. Does Abd-ru-shin wish to dispute this?*

ANSWER:

Any unaltered written record of a genuine Message of God will *always* correspond with my explanations. As also does this one. There is no contradiction here. It is only your view that is somewhat one-sided. The statement even confirms very clearly the truth of my explanations.

To possess the heritage means nothing other than to bear the ability within oneself by virtue of the spiritual origin. But as soon as man then wishes to assert his claim to this heritage, that is as soon as he wishes to enter the Spiritual Realm, then here too, as everywhere on earth, a proof is required; for any assertion of a claim at the same time calls for a proof.

The proof, however, can only be provided through the development of these abilities which he has brought with him; because in no other way can a proof be furnished for it. It becomes manifest solely through the activation of the abilities given for the purpose. But if this happens, the human spirit has also become a child of God, who is able to enter His Kingdom. The one quite automatically results from the other; for a completed development is at the same time also the power which quite automatically opens the gate to this Kingdom of Joy. But if a human being does not develop the abilities given to him in this connection, namely his heritage, he cannot assert his claim either, cannot enter the Kingdom of God, nor therefore could he become a child of God, because he buried his talent and did not invest it profitably.

Thus the words contain no contrast, no contradiction, but only a proof of the rightness of my words.

# 19

QUESTION:

*What am I to do? In the·Grail Message I have found what I have long been seeking, which has brought me great happiness. And now I am ridiculed by those around me who think differently. To avoid all quarrelling, should I give in, do everything that is required of me, and only secretly occupy myself with it inwardly?*

ANSWER:

He who has been touched by the Truth has the absolute duty also to stand up for It, otherwise he is no longer worthy of the gift of enlightenment. He should not argue and quarrel, nor perhaps try to force his conviction upon others, but calmly let all men go their own way. But he must not tolerate any attempt to divert him from his path. That which he concedes to others he has every right also to demand for himself. If, however, he makes himself the servant of the other, he deserves nothing better than that the gift be taken away from him. Christ already warned of this when He said: "He who denies me before others, him will I also deny" – that is, will not know.

How weak and paltry must the one who claims to have found the Truth through his own conviction appear to the other to whom he nevertheless bows. Can such a person gain respect for the Truth in that way? On the contrary, the mockers and scorners are only further strengthened by it, for what is precious is placed beneath their feet to be trampled and soiled. Moreover, they themselves are even prevented from recognising and valuing the Truth as such.

How very different it is when the Truth-finders face *everything* calmly, firmly, unyieldingly and resolutely. Even severely, if there is no other way to preserve the highest treasure for themselves, and save the other person from new guilt. Only through this can an opponent learn to respect a cause! Never through cowardly yielding. Many a person immediately and unscrupulously sacrifices what is most sacred within him, solely to avoid angering or offending another miserable little human being; perhaps also just to prevent his own earthly peace and comfort from being temporarily disturbed.

These are *not* the believers who will one day be permitted to enter the Kingdom of *that* God Whom they deny in such a manner. They must then join those whom they preferred to serve on earth. The time when such enforced concealment was looked upon as martyrdom is now past. It cannot be made the excuse for anything. Each one must fight for what he bears within himself, otherwise he is no longer worthy of it! It will be taken from him.

There is nothing higher than God! Beside Him *all* else must move far into the shade. No person should be forced to change his will, but in future everyone must leave alone and in peace all those who really belong to *God's people*. Henceforth not one may stretch dirty fingers towards them with impunity. He will be marked for it immediately, and perish from it. All mockery, and still more the deed, will revenge itself upon the perpetrators with totally unexpected speed and severity.

The people of the Lord at last forgather under His

banner, and remain protected. But only he who has the courage to acknowledge himself as being of this people! None else. We stand already in the beginning of this hour!

# 20

QUESTION:

*Does Abd-ru-shin know of the stigmatisation of Konnersreuth? Will he not at some time express himself to his listeners on the subject? There is so much scoffing about it.*

ANSWER:

So many questions on this subject have reached me that I really *must* deal with it.

Those who mockingly or superficially simply speak here of hysteria, and thus consider themselves wonderfully advanced, who perhaps even kindly advise putting the girl into a cold bath or sending her to some institution, possibly to a mental hospital, thus demonstrate such boundless stupidity that every second wasted on them would indeed be a pity. My answer is not intended for them! Yet it would not be an impious wish to see people of this kind subjected just once to such things for only a week. In the long run this would be the best means of making them reflect, above all of making them become a little more restrained with their frivolous "thinking and knowing", so that they are not always ready to throw stones mockingly at people like this Therese Neumann!

They would then very soon demand compassion. This is always the way. –

There certainly are mild cases who, through religious fanaticism, are able here and there to produce stigmata by auto-suggestion. But *this* case does *not* fall into any

47

such category! *That* occurrence is *not* hysteria! Let such empty prattlers talk, take no heed of them whatever. Even today it is a pity about every grain of corn that is still given them on earth to feed them; for they are empty chaff, which in the final reckoning will be considered as *naught* and scattered, parasites who stand swaggeringly in the way everywhere: fishing in murky waters after they have tried to foul even the purest waters, triumphantly sowing discord and doubt. Let us speak no more of them, for their time will not last much longer.

Thus let us consider *objectively* for once the oft-quoted *mystery of Konnersreuth!*

The suffering of the so terribly stigmatised Therese Neumann, who at times not only has to bear upon herself all the stigmata of the martyred and murdered Son of God, such as the nail marks, the spear wound, as well as the many wounds which the crown of thorns left around His head, but who has sometimes also had to live through all the physical sufferings of Christ, until in death-throes she sank back exhausted in the blood-drenched bed.

Thousands have gone on pilgrimage to the place. They pour in from all regions and all countries. Often they stand in dense crowds round the little house in which the girl has to wage her fight. During this she hears in spirit talk about the Crucifixion, in dialects of the language of that time, to the amazement of philologists.

The waiting people receive the accounts with awe; sometimes they can even have a fleeting glimpse of the sorely-afflicted girl lying in her blood; they shake their heads thoughtfully and gaze in silent astonishment at the Divine gift, as so many call it.

Science, and also the churches, find themselves confronted with a *mystery*, as they frankly admit, because they have been forced to do so by undeniable facts, this time of a *gross material* nature, which they can generally face with more confidence. This also causes their great reserve, in spite of all the sensation.

It is stated that the gratitude of all, including the church, is assured when the right solution of this apparent mystery is found.

The statement is certainly thoroughly honest and very well meant, with the best volition for what is right. But undoubtedly something was thus offered and promised which it is not really possible for men to keep to.

Again their incapacity for gratitude is due solely to the worst enemy of all spirit, to their self-chosen, absolute ruler, the earth-bound intellect!

By domination of the intellect, however, the right thing must indeed be understood. By this I do not mean some form of government, or anything like that, but simply the voluntary placing of the individual *under* his own intellect, which has brought forth all that is unhealthy in earthly conditions, and unfortunately will also continue to do so for some time yet.

But the church too, as well as all individuals, is naturally under the dreadful weight of the consequences of this hereditary sin against the spirit. Right from the beginning man has brought it in with him, without being aware of it, without suspecting or wanting it. The poisoning of all volition crept in quite unnoticed as well, and so there too the human intellect is triumphantly co-ruler. It can never be otherwise until this sin against Divine Ordinance has been thoroughly eradicated from mankind.

That also forms the barrier against the solving of this mystery of the stigmatised woman. Church and science therefore will hardly be able really to welcome the *true solution* and give thanks for it, because actual knowledge and the undimmed Truth relentlessly demand a comprehension *above* all limits of the narrow intellect! As does really any spiritual happening. Since church and science are *not* able to explain this mystery aright, this proves that despite their best volition *both parties are still so bound.* For here one fact must inseparably also follow the other.

To assert that they will still be able to do so, and to give every imaginable excuse for their inability hitherto, *is no proof.* There has been time enough for it! That it had to elapse *without* success is certainly a clear proof to the contrary. In such serious cases of suffering man must make use of every hour if he seriously wills and ... is able to! There is no time for arguments and discussions, rather is it man's duty to act. And where this does not happen there is lack of ability. This can hardly be further disputed.

But the *inability to comprehend* a true solution naturally makes an understanding impossible from the outset.

*Hence only one course remains: that facts should confirm my explanations!*

Therefore I wish here to show the course of the truth, which will lead to the solution and thus to *deliverance.* Provided that people really follow this course, and do not perhaps silently reject or counteract it for fear of being taken unawares. *But the consequence of following it would then have to give proof of the truth!*

Since following this course can do no harm in any

direction, the desire to do so cannot really be called unreasonable. Especially since through doing so many a dispute can also be settled at the same time.

Science already knows through the event itself that it too followed wrong paths in its attempts at a physical cure or alleviation. Contrary to the expected relief, soothing ointments brought about only painful inflammations, which according to reports subsided immediately the dressing was removed. That is, the wounds became clean again as soon as the medical attempts were discontinued. And this is how it is *willed*, as has already been predicted!

I would like to state explicitly that no ill-will is intended in the explanations that are necessary for clarification! I respect any sincere effort, and this has always been the case here with science as well as with the church, with the best will to help. So far no reproach can be raised concerning this, unless people now refuse to take the newly-indicated path and shrink from a proof.

In this case the whole of mankind, in regarding everything from the wrong angle, once again takes the wrong path.

Naturally the listener and reader must *think!* He must try hard really to *read* in the *events,* to *observe* calmly.

Just see how all people behave in this respect! They look for every possible thing, even for the impossible, but quite noticeably leave out *one* point, setting it entirely aside as a fairy-tale, which they never again seriously draw into the compass of the actual happening! *This one thing* is the adamantine Laws of God, is His Creative Will Which in spite of Its immutability is no longer heeded, or taken as the basis for consideration at all!

The fact speaks with *such* terrifying clarity for the inner state of men, including the churches, that this alone should be enough to make clear my descriptions of the oft-explained Fall of Man and its consequences. It can hardly come more forcibly to the recognition of deeper thinkers.

As here, so is it also in *every* instance, with every thought, every investigation, every deed! Broodingly the gaze remains fixed only on the earthly, on the lowest planes; it *can* no longer rise freely towards the height, it does not wish to! What to an unrestricted person would be the natural approach, namely first of all to consider the great Will of the Creator in everything, and to form his conclusions *only according to It*, in which alone the right solution can lie, the man of today, even representatives of the church, relegate to the realm of fantasy! This proves that they simply do not think of basing their conclusions on It. On the contrary, they quite openly yield to science, that is to the earthly intellect, to an earth-bound existence, and thus even make themselves followers of that Antichrist against whom they should warn, but whom they have never known!

*Purity of Divine Truth to the fore!* Whoever hides is no longer worthy of it. There is more at stake now than just a few human souls! What a sharp light this controversy over the Konnersreuth event throws on the steep decline in men's inner being! How clearly it reveals the actual state of *being turned away* from God and His Will! Because It is not heeded!

Likewise with those who imagine themselves to be believers. The erring human beings do not see this horror of the abyss which has already been rent open

52

within them for a long time. They continue to stagger calmly along on the brink, still held for the time being through their wrong views. Happy are all those who *learn* from this case, and who do not, for their own comfort or to conceal their lack of understanding, dismiss it in arrogant mockery as pertaining to the field of hysteria. Many even do so with real conviction, because already they are no longer able to perceive their lack of understanding and think themselves really knowing, just as a mentally deranged person even smiles at all those who do not follow his delusion. –

In her suffering Therese Neumann is often spoken of as a saint, a person specially blessed, in whose presence one prays, and for whose intercession many are probably silently longing.

And no one suspects that it is this so "favoured" one who is most in need of intercession. No one considers that it is just through her fellow-men that this poor woman is held back from a beckoning redemption! The guilt for that will unfailingly rebound also on these people who give a wrong direction to their pious worship. For through this the stigmatised person feels inwardly uplifted, as one *distinguished* by God. Through the views of the surrounding world she remains far from reflecting more seriously and deeply, from letting her thoughts and intuitive perceptions take even for once a different direction, whereby she will discover that she is not to be regarded as the *one distinguished*, but on the contrary should be a *branded one!*

The necessary humility which could lead her to deliverance is forcibly pressed into the wrong direction within her.

Therese Neumann thereby becomes a victim of the wrong attitude of her well-meaning fellow-men, unless recognition of it still comes to her in time. She passes by the opportunity for deliverance from the heavy karma in spite of its present repeated reaction, because she cannot come to recognition if things continue as they have done hitherto.

Dazzled, these spiritually blind and also spiritually deaf people stand before the house, which they see only as a sacred place; whereas in reality they are permitted likewise to experience so clearly there one of the most shattering warnings of the effect of the stern Will of God in Its immutability!

In the stigmatised woman of Konnersreuth a human soul, who in her present earthly cloak has not yet become at all clearly conscious of what is actually taking place, is struggling for deliverance. – –

The soul once reviled the Son of God on the cross! With her it is not only the first time that she has dwelt here on earth since then, and has been *so marked*.

Only if at last she becomes conscious of this, and in humility implores forgiveness, can deliverance come to her. Then she will also *behold* it *spiritually*, and thereby recognise *Him* Whose intercession can absolve her from her once so heavy guilt! The "light" which is known and familiar to her will help her in this. But nothing without her *own* recognition.

*That is the only way to her deliverance!* He who shows it to her and wishes to smooth it is the truest friend and helper; but he who denies or withholds it from her, who obstructs her in it, is her worst enemy.

Therese Neumann *herself* will see all that she needs for

deliverance as soon as she has set out on her true way inwardly, and thereupon can also regain her physical health without the help of men. – – –

The words which she has already heard from the "light" which she then sees can thus be fulfilled, because *only then* will many souls also be really helped through her suffering. Thereby many a one will yet come in time to recognition of the stern happening in the Will of God, will reflect that it is *different* from what in their easy quiescence they had previously thought, and through this will search their souls and thus attain to ascent. In no other way was the "word" of the "light" of her well-meaning guidance intended for her in the past.

Also in the words *"You may yet suffer"* lay the promise of a great blessing; for that means the new opportunity for the sufferer to make atonement through the suffering, thus perhaps still to be able to come to recognition after all, and thereby also to deliverance.

"The Saviour rejoices over it" is likewise quite right, because He rejoices over every sinner who can still be saved from eternal damnation.

Why in the world does man again grasp these words wrongly, for his own glorification?

Frivolous slaves of the intellect will perhaps feel inclined here to sneer in the usual empty fashion, without ever producing the slightest counter-evidence or a logical explanation. Especially if there is talk of reincarnation, of which indeed Germany's greatest spirits – among others, for example, Goethe – always spoke with conviction. But I wish to bring forward the *proof*, through the visible consequence which will not fail to appear as soon as the path herewith indicated is also rightly followed.

Mockers, however, would do better to be silent for the sake of their own karma; for they have no idea what they ever anew burden themselves with by it, and should wait for the proof that rests in the outcome, if ... people would really follow the path aright. I myself need do nothing in this matter. *It is possible, through a discussion, for any seriously well-meaning person to lead the thoughts of this suffering and believing one on to this path.*

If these happenings in Konnersreuth *cease* of their own accord from time to time, this still offers no solution, no healing, *much less deliverance;* for it is very likely that after a brief strengthening a *new* mystery will follow, still stronger than before, even if only after months or years! And this will bring new cogitations. If however on some pretext or another news of Therese Neumann's state of health is then withdrawn from the general public, a fatal error will again be committed with the best of intentions, and responsibilities of no small consequence incurred. –

I have already repeatedly pointed out in my lectures that the time has now come for the cycle of the former happening to close. I also mentioned that all the souls who did not accept the Message of God are again on earth for the final reckoning, at the time when the reciprocal effect of this horrible crime must set in retroactively in *full* strength.

Whosoever then reviled the Son of God in His Holy Mission as the Bringer of the Truth, whoever showed enmity and mocked Him personally of his own accord, that is of his free volition, without being compelled by his superiors or by the government, is also struck through the reciprocal action according to the gravity of his guilt. And in the course of this some must bear His marks of suffering as people thereby branded, until there can be deliverance from it or – in the case of *non-recognition* – eternal damnation, that is destruction of the *spiritual-personal* gained through development.

*All stigmatised persons have been only branded ones,* who bore a personal guilt towards the Son of God! With the exception of minor cases, which can sometimes come about through auto-suggestion in religious ecstasy. Nor could church services make any difference in this, even when the persons so afflicted lived in the most profound faith in God. But a possibility of ultimate deliverance always lay in it if they prayed in humility for forgiveness, and did not perhaps feel themselves to be saints.

This heavy karma demands redemption! It could come to them through stigmatisations, if at the same time they *recognised* a redemption in it! –

Come what may, mankind will soon have to learn to believe in the adamantine Laws of all the effects of the Divine Will, even if they have hitherto imagined and explained it differently in their secret desire. *The Love of God lies solely in the Laws which have worked immutably from the beginning of the world to this day, and will do so until the end of all days!* Christ, too, pointed out quite clearly and repeatedly that He did not wish to overthrow or to alter the Laws of God through His Message, but only to fulfil them! That is, to preserve them unchanged!

Many a gravely warning sign will yet appear before men's eyes, and in the pure Light of the Eternal Truth they will have to hear and experience many things which they have hitherto understood wrongly.

Yet in spite of all, their souls do not listen; they have eyes, and anxiously, filled with secret defiance, they close themselves to what they do not want to see. *This hiding, however, does not relieve them of any responsibility!*

# 21

*Is it not an arbitrary act when Christ on the cross said to one thief: "Today shalt thou be with me in Paradise!" After all, the thief was a criminal, and would first have to redeem his karma before he could enter Paradise.*

ANSWER:

In this incident there is neither an arbitrary act nor a contradiction. The thief on the cross of whom you speak stated quite clearly in his words that he felt guilty and deserved the punishment, whereas Christ had to suffer innocently. Thus the *full recognition of his guilt* and of a deserved punishment had awakened in him. This recognition, combined with the trusting plea that Christ should think of him when He is in His Luminous Kingdom, had the reciprocal effect of making the simultaneous suffering of the most severe earthly punishment the immediate redemption of *all* guilt. Thereby the whole karma that still threatened him could likewise be redeemed at once. Naturally the one thus freed from guilt, and thereby no longer burdened with anything, then *instantly* had to enter the Spiritual Realm, that is actually to enter Paradise, immediately after his earthly death. It was just this lawful outworking that had to bring about his instantaneous raising up to the Spiritual Realm on the falling away of the physical body. Christ's promise was therefore completely within the framework of the fulfilment of the Divine Laws, that is of the Divine Will.

Not so with the second thief, who scorned Christ in His suffering and showered Him with abuse. Here, in fulfilment of the Laws, the course of a fresh karma set in at once, which was bound to manifest in the most severe reactions in the Ethereal World, as well as later on *visibly* in his further earth-lives, and which will continue to manifest until he too comes to the recognition of his guilt, and to an honest plea for forgiveness.

# 22

QUESTION:

*Is it possible for a human soul to reincarnate at one time as a man and at another time as a woman?*

ANSWER:

The incarnation of a soul with regard to sex depends upon its characteristics. If the characteristics of a soul so change that what is masculine alters and gradually inclines more to the feminine nature, or vice versa, then it does happen that this soul is incarnated at one time as a man and at another time as a woman. But this only concerns the earthly body. The human spirit always remains what it decided to be at the beginning of its wanderings through Creation.

# 23

QUESTION:

*Are all the questions which are sent in answered?*

ANSWER:

No. From the way many readers ask questions it can often be perceived that they are far from grasping the deep seriousness of the Grail Message; because in most cases the questions are about things the knowledge of which does not in the least contribute to the spiritual ascent of a human being's personal ego, but can serve merely to satisfy the urge for intellectual knowledge.

But the human spirits who really wish to save themselves *have no more time left* for such practices as have hitherto prevailed! The Grail Message therefore gives only what the human spirit needs to make the necessary ascent easier for itself, indeed to make it possible at all.

Anyone who only to some extent perceives the urgency for this, instead of putting all the questions will exert the whole strength of his intuitive perception in trying to fathom and absorb what is *given* in the Message. What he cannot yet understand, however, he will not reject or pass by, but he will look within himself to see whether the cause for his inability to understand does not lie in some corner there. –

Every question is a demand! If it concerns what is necessary for spiritual ascent, then it is justified. But if it seeks merely to facilitate intellectual satisfaction, then it is a presumption in face of the seriousness of the Message, because such things concern far lesser and lower matters than is the purpose and content of the Message.

But he who occupies himself with It seriously enough, putting aside any prejudice in doing so, must also find the answer to *every intellectual question* in what is given. If he *cannot* do so, then either his intellect is not adequate for it, or he has not gone deep enough.

From the first to the last lecture, the Message must naturally be taken *as a whole*, otherwise it is impossible to grasp It, and persistent effort and spiritual diligence are needed for this! So far only what is absolutely necessary has been given, because time presses irresistibly to know the most urgent things. It leaves no room for unnecessary delay. For this reason some questions must be disregarded. After the first great purification they will still be answered, together with many other detailed explanations.

The lectures of the Message do not beg the favour of men, they do not solicit in order to be bought for the sake of profit, as of course is always the case with books, but they are *given!* This means that they stand calmly in the midst of everything, entirely on their own, indifferent to their surroundings, but *living*, and not to be pushed away by the masses, to whom they can say nothing because these are not yet willing; nor can they be destroyed by the hatred of those to whom they seem irksome.

Everything and everyone will some day have to take into account what is said in them. He cannot pass quietly by, without searchingly measuring his "ego" against them. The words are not for discussion, and do not ask for opinions; but they are given, and they will endure, firmer than rock, harder than steel, immutable and relentless. – –

# 24

*In many quarters it is now affirmed that Christ was an avowed vegetarian. What does Abd-ru-shin say about this?*

ANSWER:

I need say nothing about it, but only point out that Christ observed the eating of the Paschal lamb. Moreover I would refer to the well-known feeding of the five thousand, when He Himself had *fish* handed to the people, and therefore was by no means in favour of eating *only* vegetables. Christ really should not be used for the propaganda purposes of some movement.

# 25

QUESTION:

*After studying the Grail Message I have come in the course of my reflections to regard the Material World as the real Creation. Is there anything to be said against this?*

ANSWER:

Everything! For such a view is wrong, and is not taken from the Grail Message. In further lectures I shall in any case gradually penetrate more and more deeply into the hitherto-existing mysteries of Creation, and in doing so shall have to divide it into ever more different sections, drawing it apart, whereby also ever more gradations, which cannot be given during the first comprehensive survey, will naturally appear.

Thus in answering this question I would like at least to mention in advance that the actual Creation is *only the Spiritual Realm*, that is Paradise. All other things are *consequences*, replicas which become ever weaker. So for example the direct Work of the Divine Will, thus of the Holy Spirit, is *solely* the Primordial Spiritual Sphere, which however bears within it all that it needs to work on automatically with the Power that lies in the Primordial Spiritual, through the Primordial Beings, that is the *directly* Created Ones, who thereby become mediators for the coming-into-being of the further Creation. All that is beyond the Primordial Spiritual Realm is therefore not created *directly* by the Divine Will, but only indirectly, that is to say with His Power, which was placed into the Primordial Spiritual through the mediation of the Primordial Beings.

Those human beings who have already often said to me: "I do want to be good. If I am not it is not my fault. Why did not God create me so that I can only be good?" will see from the foregoing how wrong is this thought of theirs.

# 26

*Is mysticism more useful for spiritual ascent than, for instance, occultism and spiritism? Of what use are the numerous sects for it?*

ANSWER:

When you are faced with such a question you must first of all seek to penetrate the spiritual results of the various activities with your intuitive perception, and form your opinion *according to that alone*. You will find that the "mystic" by no means stands higher, but is just as harmful as the spiritist and occultist, and in the final analysis also the sects. –

Many decades ago the unfortunate inmates of brothels came mainly from the circles of shopgirls and domestic servants. Very often the unhappy cause of this came from an inner urge to experience a freer and more colourful life, or on the other hand from the trust arising out of love for some man, who in his fickle conduct or frivolity was quite incapable of honouring such trust. Only rarely was there a definite personal propensity for a base and frivolous mode of life. The moral decline of such girls, who in the end can no longer summon the strength to get out of this swamp, is well known.

Incidents quite similar to those of the past are now also widespread in the spiritual field. The urge to penetrate the so-called life in the beyond, which many a person imagines to be quite different from what it is, today leads great masses of so-called seekers, who long

67

for something different, *towards the swamp of the Darkness.*

Just as the girls who inwardly long for something better, or even only something new and hitherto unknown to them, will not recognise the falseness of the men who court them, because this would be almost tantamount to giving up many a wish, so little do the often frenzied spiritual seekers see that instead of genuine gold ... they adorn themselves with tinsel and baubles, which deludes them into thinking they have risen higher. Wrapped in a delusion, they go self-satisfied through their life on earth, and then in the beyond remain poor dupes of that delusion, which they must naturally take over with them, and which dominates them there.

They all are caught in the World of Matter, and do not find the strength to tear themselves out of the tenacity of this delusion, because they dare not adjust their intuitive perception differently for fear of losing something that has become dear to them.

They are irretrievably abandoned to ruin; with the coming disintegration of all matter they will also meet with the disintegration of their previously hard-won *personal* consciousness, and because they *cannot be used in a conscious state* they will be relegated to formlessness.

That, however, is *not* progress, as Buddhists have assumed, but an extinction of the development so far achieved, because this has gone in the wrong direction.

Now what the unscrupulous youths and men who bring about such an unhappy crisis are in the experiences of craving girls and women, is today represented in the spiritual field by the numerous societies and sects of religion, of occultists, spiritists and whatever else of the kind has formed. They are the worst soul-catchers for the Darkness!

Yet those who deem themselves leaders very often even have the volition for what is good! And in time this volition could also bring absolutely nothing but good if there were not one great hindrance here, which in every case shows itself to be much stronger, and everywhere diverts the best volition from the right course. It is the rejection of all that does not accord with the individual leaders' own ideas. The rejection comes from an instinctive fear that they would indeed have to change many a thing in the course they themselves have so far taken, as a result of which the adherents might possibly realise how they often follow entirely wrong paths. In *this* realisation some of the reverence which they show so unconditionally towards their "masters" might then be lost.

Foolish as this thought is, it nevertheless causes many leaders to stumble, and makes them persist in following their course, although sometimes it intuitively dawns on them that they are doing wrong thereby.

But not only the leaders are to be reproached for this; for the *adherents themselves* cause still greater harm to themselves and their fellow-adherents on the same course. If perhaps the founder of some movement really had a right goal, and wanted to lead his followers towards the Truth, it can safely be assumed that inwardly his followers would always lag very far behind the teaching itself. Once the founder has passed over, the want of truly experiencing a good teaching would often be very soon revealed. The adherents imagined that in the teaching they already had the whole and the highest, and through this they succumbed to spiritual arrogance, which closed the door to the possibility of further ascent. Jubilant, they pass unsuspectingly by the ultimate Truth, for which their own founder only wished to prepare them. That is why many a right course is inevitably doomed by its adherents, instead of leading to the Luminous Height.

How many seekers, and those who thought they knew, unsuspectingly passed by the only real Master, the Son of God, at that time. Above all those who considered themselves qualified to recognise His coming. Just those even became His bitterest enemies. Why do people not learn from this?

Today we see the Christians living in many wrong interpretations of their Master's teaching. Proud, arrogant, and yet devoid of understanding in the face of the deep Truth that lies in the Message of Christ.

*This* alone makes it possible for the many sects and societies to flourish, because the human spirit is aware of a fierce inner compulsion rising up, *to the effect* that it needs *more* than the churches give it in their monotonous, superficial interpretations.

People hope to receive greater clarity in these sects and societies, and indeed are often satisfied if it sounds *different* from the churches. The urge makes them already see progress in this, even if in reality it is much less than they have already received in the churches.

For example, one who takes part in a spiritist seance only too easily mistakes what is interesting and *novel* for what is *valuable*. It does not occur to him that what is interesting need not necessarily at the same time be valuable. Not one reflects with calm objectivity *how* all this is really to benefit his own spiritual *ascent*, where merely his inner quality alone is finally decisive! He is proud of being on intimate terms with those who have passed over! Yet in reality it is not in any way different from how it is with his fellow-men here on earth. He too, and every human being on earth, has within him the body that is worn by those who have passed on. Only the gross material cloak is still over it. And what he allows himself to be told with great effort by those in the beyond is not the thousandth part of what Christ brought.

In spite of this he places a greater value on all these petty revelations, with whose contents he has long been completely familiar. What a lack of independent thinking and intuitive perceiving he thereby reveals in his entire being.

Nor does he then use what he experiences in these seances to fathom Christ's Message in all seriousness as quickly as possible, and learn to understand It aright, to grasp Its whole greatness, in order to swing himself up to the spiritual freedom which is intended therein; but on the contrary he clings to what is offered to him in this pettiness, just because it has a different outward form.

It is a *further hindrance*, and no advancement!

One of the greatest mediators for the Darkness is *conceit!* Let us look at spiritists. With very few exceptions the adherents suffer from such boundless conceit, which they clothe in apparent humility of knowledge, that one simply cannot speak with them without feeling disgust and being repelled by it. They imagine they can "help" many departed ones, whereas in reality they themselves are in far greater need of help. Unfortunately this is something that is to be found almost everywhere. This morbid will to help, however, is by no means love, nor does it spring from the great desire to serve; and just as little can it be attributed to a purely human readiness to help, and even less to true piety, but it is nothing other than the most unpleasant inner presumption, which cannot be eradicated.

And the Darkness makes full use of this greatest of all weaknesses, especially in the circles of beginner-mediums. A dark one appears, lamenting about something or other, and instantly the ignorant little human beings want to "help" this poor soul. With a pious look in their eyes, prayers, holy water, charms and words of incantation, which express nothing more than just the boundless arrogance of those who think they know.

It is a self-satisfying comedy, nothing else. Self-adulation! They flatter themselves. The help lies solely in the imagination. *In many cases the dark one does not want help!* He knows very well that these people cannot help him, and simply relies on thus dragging them down to himself unnoticed! Just as anything dark always pounces only on weaknesses. And with great prospect of success; because through wanting to help, those who are thus inclined open themselves to the currents of the Darkness. They hold out their hand to this person in the beyond to draw him up, but thereby come into contact with him, and sink without realising it!

The fact that they intend otherwise can be of absolutely no benefit to them in this case; for they voluntarily expose themselves to these dangers, from which otherwise they would be completely protected. As it is, however, they themselves break through the protection, and such recklessness must avenge itself.

Even when such people, as soon as they get into difficulties through their foolishness and cannot proceed further, finally need and ask for help from others, they always want as help only the satisfaction of their own wishes, and not perhaps liberation from the dark spirit which they had drawn to themselves.

Now if to such a circle there came a true helper, who instead of satisfying their wrong wishes sent one belonging to the Darkness to where according to its nature it belongs, to prevent it from dragging credulous ignorant people into perdition, all those liberated would oppose this helper in united hostility, and probably call him a messenger of the Darkness, when all of a sudden their "poor" spirit was no longer able to come. They do not see that in reality it is simply anger at the loss of many an entertaining hour in which they could be "elevated".

The "pious" call it harshness, un-Christian, when such a spirit is despatched to where it came from, because *only there* and nowhere else can it come to recognition. In order really to help a low spirit, things totally different from what the participants and leaders of spiritist circles can offer are actually needed.

For these and many other reasons besides, it is pointless to say even one word to such erring ones in their conceit; although with such incidents I could readily produce proofs in *any* seance, no matter where or by whom led, even in the most powerful ones. But where really serious volition is concerned, people will always find me ready. I will confront *any* spiritist circle or its spirits, *any* demon or other oppressors, without hesitation! –

It is no different with occultists who, while seeking and to some extent experimenting, become lost in matters which chain them even more to the lower ethereal surroundings. The currents to which they open themselves simply bind them more firmly, and hold them back. –

Equally great harm is caused by the works of mystics, who with their uncertain groping lead into a maze of perplexity, and to becoming lost in it in the natural course of events. For the most part it is fantasy and over-enthusiasm in which they seek to indulge themselves, or else they wish to give the impression of real knowledge, which however only resembles the meaningful smile of an ignoramus. It is neither more nor less than just a delusion in which they live, and which sometimes also tempts them to ridicule others who are less dangerous.

They are not even aware of being dangerous themselves, because this lies *only* in the spiritual field, which they are incapable of recognising. *Personally* they are really quite harmless, but *their works* cause frightful havoc and lead people astray, whether they carefully clothe their fantastic thoughts in novels, or mould them into other forms. Mysticism leads even more easily into the embrace of dark currents, because at the same time it brings with it a somnolent ease or even a pleasurable eeriness, but it timidly shuns all clarity. The human spirits thereby exist in an *unhealthy* life, without a firm foothold, and are pulled hither and thither.

But God wishes His Laws to be obeyed, because *only in doing so* can people become happy! This obedience, however, *requires complete knowledge,* no obscurities. Indeed all life and movement in Creation is subject to the Laws, and comes about through them. Therefore people *must* recognise Creation *clearly* and in *full consciousness,* right down to the smallest parts! Where then is there any room left for mysticism? Mysticism in Creation is *contrary to the Divine Will,* it does not accord with the Commandments of God, and must therefore harm those whom people seek to talk into it.

Thus mystics are closely related to occultists and spiritists, and do harm through the consequences of their activities. *Spiritually* there is no difference between them.

In addition very many *religious* sects and societies are to be pitied, all of which imagine that each by itself alone has the whole Truth and is striding *ahead* of all the others. *Everything* they encounter they confront with this preconceived notion; they do not enter into other thoughts, examining them afresh and with an alert mind, but drag with them everything out of the past. As soon as the old cannot be blended with what is new, they reject the new as wrong. They adjust their standards to the old which was given to them, and which they often did not even understand aright.

Under this restraint their judgment is always hasty and obstinate. It is prejudiced; and not with their own words but with those of others, which they themselves have never rightly understood, they seek to dispose of everything as inferior in comparison with *their* knowledge. For this they use sanctimonious phrases, which at once not only indicate spiritual arrogance, but also show a real inner emptiness and rigid narrow-mindedness.

These are the hosts who always call quite familiarly: "Lord, Lord!" But the Lord will not know them! Beware first and foremost of *these* "believers", so that you do not apathetically run into perdition with them. –

# 27

QUESTION:

*Is Abd-ru-shin opposed to astrology?*

ANSWER:

No! On the contrary, I know very well the great value of astrology. But equally well also the deficiencies of the present knowledge concerning it. For this reason I advise the many who work in it, and who are very well aware of its deficiencies, never to withhold this fact from those who ask for their counsel. But the greatest danger again lies, as with nearly all such things, on the side of the public who seek advice! The greater part of them become so timidly dependent that they no longer dare make any free decision whatever, thus rendering a spiritual ascent, a spiritual maturing, impossible for themselves. I would very much like to help smooth the path for genuine astrology to the height which is its due.

# 28

QUESTION:

*After the interest of an unusually large number of people had been aroused, the Konnersreuth case was suddenly withdrawn from the public without a satisfactory explanation of the surely extraordinary occurrence being given by those authorities who brought about this withdrawal. The Konnersreuth case has developed into a question that concerns humanity, and therefore should not remain just a behind-the-scenes study by a few who imagine themselves called for it. And this in the year 1927, and not perhaps a hundred years earlier! Should not a general protest then be raised?*

ANSWER:

Do you think that you will get many *valuable* followers with a protest today? Already from the beginning I have foreseen this withdrawal, and have also even drawn attention to it! A sign that I have recognised rightly, because ignorance when embarrassed can hardly act otherwise, unless it has the courage to admit ignorance. Just wait calmly for the end, even if it should take years. The truth will finally reveal itself also in the earthly sense, in spite of concealment. The explanations hitherto attempted by so many who pretend to know have been for the greater part only the most desultory fantasies, extracts compiled from books read but hardly understood; and even science and the church have been unable to offer anything satisfactory. No wonder that it causes disquietude when in the confusion thus created such an obvious retreat is suddenly undertaken. Yet there is no need to be agitated. One day the hour of clarification will come. I shall *then* have no need to delete one sentence from my explanation of the Konnersreuth case or add one to it, although today, with but few exceptions, people will probably still only try with a smile to make light of it. For my part the Konnersreuth case is closed.

# 29

QUESTION:

*What is energy? And what is gravity?*

ANSWER:

These questions are premature; for they will be dealt with fully only in later lectures. However, I will answer them by giving at least a very brief outline.

*Energy is spirit!* I must still go much more into the actual subject of spirit; for spirit embraces almost *all* the unsolved questions of our present-day science. Spirit also has many gradations, which could not be taken into account until now because nobody knows it, for "spirit" has not yet been recognised by this mankind at all.

Spirit is so many-sided in its gradations that in these many gradations it has brought forth all the errors about which men still rack their brains in vain.

What the exact sciences have called energy is therefore spirit. Not, however, the kind of spirit from which the self-conscious human spirit formed itself, but a *different* kind.

Today just briefly this about it: The Primordial Beings radiate in the Spiritual Creation, that is in Paradise, *in their volition*. These radiations are *also* spiritual, but a gradation downwards; because they are not direct radiations of the Holy Spirit, of the Divine Will, *but radiations* of the *Primordial Beings* created through the Holy Spirit! As a spiritual gradation downwards, these radiations now surge across the boundary of the Spiritual Realm like rays, and stream through the other parts of the Universe; but in spite of the gradation, being spiritual they still carry within them living power, which has not only a thrusting and pressing but also a magnetically-attracting effect on a different non-spiritual environment.

The magnetic attraction-power of these spiritual currents, however, is not of such great strength as that of Primordial Creation, which holds the entire Universe. Thus it is that the currents forced out from the Spiritual Realm can always draw to themselves *only small particles* of a different environment, and are thereby covered by them, which process divides the originally uniform currents. Such a spiritual current is thereby split into innumerable minute particles in the natural course of events, because the coverings of what has been attracted have a separating effect. These coverings, however, are only very minute, thin layers of the various kinds of environment, because the *individual* small spiritual particle of a current has also only a weak magnetic holding-power, corresponding to its minuteness. In this way electrons, atoms, etc., gradually come into being.

But the way there is infinitely long. This too I shall briefly outline today. Picture to yourselves: The radiations of the Primordial Beings, in their activity of volition, press beyond the boundary of Paradise. They enter the Animistic Realm as magnetically-attracting strangers. The animistic itself again consists of many gradations, which for the time being I want first to classify into *three* basic species only: into *Fine, Medium* and *Gross* Animistic Substance, quite apart from the basic kinds of Conscious Animistic Substance as the highest of this kind, and Unconscious Animistic Substance.

As the spiritual current enters the fine species of Animistic Substance, the covering, called forth by the magnetic power of the current, takes place at once through this Fine Animistic Substance, whereby at the same time an eager movement immediately sets in. This process of covering appears as though a hostile army is falling upon this intruder, the spiritual current, whereas in reality it is only the spiritual element, in this alien nature of its new environment, that causes the movement through its inherent magnetic attraction-power. Thus attracted, the animistic rushes towards the spiritual at breakneck speed. Simultaneously with the process of covering, the dispersal of the current takes place. There is no intermingling of the spiritual with Fine Animistic Substance, but only a covering of the spiritual by Animistic Substance. The core is a spiritual particle, covered all over with Fine Animistic Substance, which is held by the magnetic attraction-power of the spiritual core.

In spite of the covering, however, the spiritual core retains its magnetic radiation, and penetrates the fine animistic covering with it. But during this penetration warmth is generated, and a change takes place in the radiation of the spiritual particle. Through the connection, the radiation comes forth different from what it was at first, and in this change it acquires an influence on *Medium* Animistic Substance.

At the same time, through the process of the attracting of Fine Animistic Substance, a compression of the individual components of Fine Animistic Substance in the covering, thus an accumulation around each spirit particle, has taken place; and this compressed accumulation brings about a reduction in volume of a specific compound in relation to the other still free-floating loose environment of Fine Animistic Substance. As a result, this compound is no longer held by the attraction-power of the Spiritual Realm, of Paradise, at the *same* height as the parts that are still loose. With this compression there is a *further withdrawal from the always uniformly-working magnetic power-station* that rests in the nature of *Spiritual* Creation, of Paradise. *And this process is the beginning of the Law of Gravity.* At the same time it is a turning-point in the motive power of what has happened up to then.

The process must be keenly observed: Through the activity of the volition of the Primordial Beings, radiations come into being. But mark well: These radiations are not the volition itself, but only accompanying factors of the volition, *secondary effects* of the main stream of a volition. Nevertheless these side effects, unchecked by the originator, still receive so much thrusting-power that they are *forced beyond* the boundary of the Spiritual Realm, and there, through the magnetic attraction-power inherent in them by virtue of their spiritual nature, they bring about the effect which I have just described. The main stream of the volition of the Primordial Beings has nothing to do with this; it always directly affects only the intended goal. Much more powerfully, more consciously. I shall speak about this some other time.

The instantaneous covering of the spiritual particles forced across the boundary immediately prevents them from flowing back automatically into the Spiritual, because the layer of Fine Animistic Substance thrusts itself in between, or rather, is held in between by the spirit particles' inherent attraction-power. Thus the first process of withdrawal from the magnetic centre was one of being forced out as a side-effect of some conscious volition. With the first covering, however, something contrary at once sets in as the originator of the onward movement: the having-to-distance-itself-further through the condensation of Fine Animistic Substance due to attraction, in relation to the hitherto-existing environment of the other still uncondensed Fine Animistic Substance. From then onwards *several* factors always contribute to the urge for movement. With each further covering a new factor is added.

Here again it must be interpolated that every single species in the whole of Creation is individually adjusted in a quite specific degree, stipulated by its nature, to the attraction-power of Spiritual Creation, fundamentally always attuned to the *loose, unconnected*, thus *not compressed* particular species.

Ethereal Matter is therefore adjusted to a different degree of the attraction-power from Gross Matter. But in turn also different from Animistic Substance. Thus it is that, with the covering of the spirit particle through compression of Fine Animistic Substance, a different degree immediately sets in for the attraction-power of the Spiritual Creation, which allows the covered spirit particle to move further from the point of attraction.

This process is repeated with each new covering. It is called the Law of Gravity, which actually is anchored in the particular possibility for every thing to move further away from the natural attraction-power of the Spiritual Creation! This possibility of moving further away is subject to the particular consistency in its various changes.

84

With regard to further progress I can be more brief: The compressed covering of Fine Animistic Substance brings with it, under the above-mentioned effects, what according to our concepts is called *sinking*, whereby it approaches Medium Animistic Substance, for which by this time the radiation of the spirit, which has been changed by the covering, has again just as magnetic an effect as the spiritual particle previously had on Fine Animistic Substance. Here again it should be noted that the direct, thus the unchanged radiation of the spirit particle, could not affect Medium Animistic Substance as strongly as the radiation that has been *changed* by the covering of Fine Animistic Substance. *Only this* can have such an attracting effect on Medium Animistic Substance that it immediately places itself as a further covering over the covering of Fine Animistic Substance, and is held by the changed attraction-power of the spirit particle.

With this begins the same process as in Fine Animistic Substance, and here too the radiation of the spirit particle is once again changed in that it is influenced by the *two* coverings. So it goes on into Gross Animistic Substance, thence into Fine, Medium and Gross Ethereal Matter, again and again receiving new coverings of the various species, until eventually it enters Fine Gross Matter, therewith placing *that* covering around it. From there it proceeds into Medium Gross Matter, and only then into Heavy, that is Coarse Gross Matter, which in its loose state corresponds absolutely to the gross matter of our body and our visible surroundings. But it is only here that they now become all that is known to the present-day exact sciences – electrons, atoms, etc.

The driving energy, however, is only *the core* in everything, the minute *spirit particle,* which as the lowest gradation in the Spiritual Realm belongs only to the secondary manifestations of the volition of the Primordial Beings in the so-called Paradise, the Spirit-Centre of Creation.

As it is presented, the description is naturally still very one-sided; and practical application can only be derived from what is stated when the Laws of Homogeneity are also applied. In doing so the *coverings* must first of all be considered; for each covering is subject only to the Laws of *its species,* which is equivalent to saying that the spirit particle can only operate aright where its particular *outermost* covering is within its homogeneous species. Thus with the gross material covering, only in Gross Matter, and there too only in the very definite particular species. With its ethereal covering, only in the homogeneous species of Ethereal Matter. In the animistic covering, only in the particular species of Animistic Substance.

Hence it naturally follows that what we have designated as the Law of Gravity, namely the possibility of moving further from the attraction-power of the Spiritual Realm, always predominantly affects only the particular outer covering, that this is therefore decisive for the whereabouts and for the strength of the direct activity. The *keys* to open the gates into other species, as from Fine into Medium and Gross Animistic Substance, as also then into the Worlds of Matter, are the *changes* in the *radiations* of the spirit particle, which always arise through further coverings. Without these changes neither a transition nor an activity through attraction would be possible. What is spiritual would therefore have to remain completely ineffective if it came directly into the World of Matter without a transition, because through this there would be no possibility of any connection.

Finally one thing more: It therefore follows from my explanation that the spiritual by itself is *not subject to the Law of Gravity!* It knows no weight, and as soon as its coverings are detached will always *have* to ascend or fly irresistibly upwards, into the Spiritual Realm, which is not subject to the Law of Gravity as we know it.

To avoid errors, I wish to point out that the spirit seed-grain of man is a *totally different species* of the spiritual from the spirit-currents described here. More-over, it has much more power of attraction, and also exercises this to a certain degree directly on the covered spirit-particles. Many a listener will now be able to imagine that the nonetheless vast diffusion of *spiritual* species in Subsequent Creation, hence also in our parts, in being freed from the heaviness of the environment carry within them a tremendous buoyancy towards their spiritual origin; and thus, combined with the attraction-power coming from there, help to give the entire Universe *that support,* and to stipulate that course, to which everything must adhere.

The field is so vast that today's small survey must be divided into many lectures in order to introduce the listeners and readers properly. But in spite of the apparent complexity, in the end everything only comes back again to the utmost simplicity. The deviation of the human spirit alone, through the suppression of its *spiritual receptive ability*, forces me to lead the listeners over years of lectures through the wearisome trails of the intellectual ways, because everyone, without exception, has become lost in the undergrowth.

The massing of the described particles into celestial bodies, with the resulting accumulation of magnetic power of the spiritual contained therein, which in addition to the great power-centre of the Spiritual Realm acting on them have in turn among and within them their own – and naturally in comparison with the Spiritual Realm far weaker – centres of attraction, which in the great distance from Paradise as the main centre can also work separately among themselves, although they always remain suspended in the influence of the main attraction-power of the Spiritual Paradise, will be a series of lectures by itself. Likewise the massing into human, animal and plant bodies.

Knowledge is power! This is a much-used saying, but for this a different knowledge is needed from what people imagine they already possess today. It is *spiritual* knowledge, not merely intellectual knowledge! The exact sciences have not hitherto achieved anything special in this, and all others lose themselves with uncertain groping in the realm of the countless deficiencies of the lower regions. Only he who knows *all* the mysteries of Creation can bring the World of Matter to blossom, or lay it in ruins.

# 30

QUESTION:

*Is it possible for human beings to be able to see earlier or later incarnations with the aid of photographs?*

ANSWER:

Certainly. But not without some limitations. It will be difficult with such people as are in some way directly interwoven with great world events (thus not only in the earthly sense); for these stand under specially strong currents, which confuse a seer or cloud his vision, perhaps even make an approach impossible for his own good.

# 31

QUESTION:

*Is Abd-ru-shin a seer, or does he draw from extraneous sources?*

ANSWER:

Although this question is really a purely personal one, thus arising from curiosity, and knowing about it can contribute absolutely nothing towards spiritual ascent, I will make an exception for once and answer it.

I am not a seer in the accepted sense, nor on the other hand do I draw from extraneous sources. I have no need of either. Nor do I borrow from other quarters, as some imagine. There is no compiling from the endeavours of others. Should you find related trends in various old and newer teachings, it is simply because these carry grains of truth in them. Such must indeed remain constant everywhere, and therefore will also be found in my lectures.

*I myself draw*, and do not compile! He who cannot be satisfied with that would not understand it, even if I were to explain more. I wish people *to examine the words* and absorb them as far as they are able, for without the *personal conviction* of each individual it has no value for him at all. The conviction, however, must not be because of the Bringer of the Word, but must come from an inner accord with what is said! I have already mentioned this emphatically at the beginning of my lectures, and moreover this I *demand*. In view of that such questions are superfluous. And besides, he who in reading does not himself intuitively sense the drawing has not yet fully grasped the Message either.

# 32

QUESTION:

*Since Abd-ru-shin explains the mystery of Konners-reuth with such certainty, perhaps he can also say who this soul was in former times, whence its karma originates?*

ANSWER:

Of course I can. The reason I have been silent is simply that I keep to *objective* statements, and do not draw anything into the personal. To clarify a public question I only touch upon what is absolutely necessary.

# 33

QUESTION:
*Can a person possessed by a demon be healed?*

ANSWER:

A human being cannot be "possessed" by a demon at all! This is impossible, for quite natural reasons alone; because the core of the human being is *spirit,* but a demon is an entity, once harmless, yet nourished through the volition of the human spirit till it became a demon. And since spirit is higher than an entity in its consistency, the entity is unable even temporarily to push aside the spirit, a necessary condition for possession. However, the human being can be demoniacally *influenced!* That is a very different thing; for in order to be influenced the person concerned must be deliberately accommodating inwardly, whether occasioned through his action, thus a process working from without inwards, or through his own volition, some propensity which he has acquired and thus turned into a characteristic. In this case he first opens himself inwardly to this evil influence, and then works under the influence towards the outside.

To be demoniacally influenced, therefore, cannot happen without one's own volition. For *this* reason a cure or help is *made very difficult.* This condition is also much more dangerous for man himself and for his surroundings, because he acts in a more calculating, malicious way, in full consciousness.

A possessed person, however, is intermittently or continuously really "possessed" by a malicious, low, thus dark human spirit in the beyond. This means that during the period of possession his own spirit within him is pushed aside and paralysed, while the intruder takes possession, even though only in part, of the body and its brain function, but completely so of the day brain. This crowding-out can take place because the evil one is also spirit, therefore not an entity, but ever again only where the person's *own* spirit has given the possibility for it. This can happen in various ways. Either through too great a laxity, that is, indolence of his own spirit, or by dallying with those in the beyond, as through table-turning, etc., as well as through a number of other happenings, such as shock, fright or fear, a condition which for brief moments paralyses the strength of the person's own spirit.

But here again there are so many variations in the process that it cannot be answered according to a plan or only cursorily. I would have to write a special lecture about it, but today I only present the rough outline, which can give the right picture to those who ask about it.

Being possessed can be cured easily and quickly. Naturally not by spiritists, not by clergymen, not by exorcism and the like, nor by those with a part knowledge – all that is of no account in Creation – but it must lie in the power of one called for it, which is far stronger than that of all the malicious spirits concerned, who often have an enormous energy at their disposal. But just as these evil ones receive additional strength from the Darkness, so a pure spirit in pure faith receives powers from what is luminous and pure in addition to his own, through the simplest prayer before acting. –

Being possessed can thus be quickly cured, being influenced with much greater difficulty. It can safely be assumed that very many people in mental institutions are only possessed, not ill. In time they will naturally perish physically in the process; for the body is unable to endure this excessive spiritual pressure for any length of time. –

# 34

QUESTION:

*How is it that Christ has never said anything about reincarnation? Nor has He ever spoken of the Holy Grail.*

ANSWER:

Christ spoke only of all those things that people of *His time* needed to know to enable them to ascend spiritually, nothing more. But today people must have more detailed explanations, because they have indeed shown themselves to be incapable of grasping the deep meaning of the parables and illustrations given in simplicity by Christ. Apart from that, however, the Last Supper at the end of His time on earth was a *Grail Act*.

But these explanations go beyond what is necessary now. What men need *today* for ascent they have received. Whoever wants to know still more has not recognised what has been said so far, and anything further could not help him either. –

# 35

QUESTION:

*Abd-ru-shin speaks of the Universal Law of the Attraction-Power of Homogeneous Species. How is it then that extremes make contact, whereas like poles repel each other? This can be observed everywhere, even among human beings. Good wives on the whole do not really have special husbands, while good husbands often have remarkably bad wives, and so on. Many such examples could be quoted.*

ANSWER:

When I speak of the Universal Law of the Attraction-Power of Homogeneous Species, it is not a matter of small part-species like those referred to in the question. If you wish to speak of homogeneous species in the Universal Law you must first be clear about what a *species* really is!

Positive electricity, for instance, as well as a bad wife or a bad husband, is by no means a species of its own, such as takes effect in the Universal Law. Positive and negative parts crowd together, because only with many other parts can they form a species, which then exercises the power of attraction on the similar *united* species. Moreover, the crowding together of the various part-species is a direct effect of this Law of the Attraction-Power of Homogeneous Species, which compels the parts belonging to a complete species to find one another and unite. In any case, I shall come to these things later on, the nearer we approach to the earthly visible happenings.

# 36

*Abd-ru-shin's words about spiritists are of such sever-*
*ity that one can actually assume only two things behind*
*them. Either still a partial ignorance on the subject, or*
*such a transcendent knowledge that it stands even above*
*all those in the beyond who manifest in spiritist circles.*
*Only one of these two things can form the basis of his*
*really striking severity, which is in direct contrast to the*
*other lectures. Why is Abd-ru-shin such a stern opponent*
*of spiritism, which is so widespread?*

ANSWER:

I am not an opponent of spiritism. Already once have
I specially stressed this. But the *interpretation and atti-*
*tude of the spiritists* must, with a few exceptions, be
rejected. They could be compared to a flock of sheep
without shepherds, but in reality they are far worse off
than these, as will very soon become evident.

Spiritism in itself has full justification and a high task.
In most cases the manifestations from the so-called
beyond are well-meant, and in their somewhat narrow
view they are completely suited to the rather limited
comprehending-power of those who thirst for them. If
the comprehending-power of the circles referred to were
healthier and freer, the revelations could be given reciprocally through those in the beyond who have already
*risen to a higher level.*

But here, too, what is wrong and reprehensible is only
brought in by the adherents, that is by the spiritists,

because each circle imagines that it receives the highest, the pure Truth, which however is still completely unknown, or at least obscured, to the very ones who manifest.

In reply to the above question I freely state that it is not ignorance that makes me speak thus, but *knowing more* than *all* the spiritist circles and those who manifest to them!

Calmly and coolly I assert that where the highest things seem to reveal themselves – of course always only in the opinion of these circles – lies a boundless error, called forth, cultivated and nourished by the adherents of these circles themselves. People simply do not know what a confusion of ideas they continually succumb to. And it is *this* that gives them the *impression* of being so inwardly secure.

I do not dispute with them their good faith in themselves, and in the high nature of all the manifestations in which they take part, but in all severity and quite categorically I do dispute with them the real knowledge of either side: of the adherents and also of those who manifest!

Well-meant and sincere as they are, the letters received from various nations and countries are distressing evidence to me that things are much worse in these matters than I care to say. One can only turn away in great sorrow from all those who have gone astray, who owing to their own limitations feel so inwardly comforted and uplifted. It is just in this apparent upliftment that the frightful danger of destruction lies, which now no longer even threatens, but is already completely inevitable. It is not conceit in those concerned, of whom there are millions, nor an intentional presumption, but it is with pity for others in their hearts that they take the road to their own damnation. –

Here too I can only say: Wait just the short time, which is not long enough to tire anybody, and many a one of them will at last recognise with great horror that through his own behaviour the way before him is still so long that he does not now have enough strength left to reach the longed-for goal just before the last hour, because he has delayed far too long only over trivialities, which he stubbornly held to be great and sacred.

# 37

QUESTION:

*I use a pendulum! Not in the ordinary way, but in serious investigation. I know that I can rely absolutely on my results. So, in addition to many others, I have also used the pendulum in connection with Christ, Moses and Buddha, with striking results. Finally I did not even forbear to use the pendulum also with regard to Abd-ru-shin, and know from this who he is. Besides myself, I know many people gifted in other ways who likewise have this knowledge, and hold firmly to their conviction of it.*

*In his reply to the question of whether he is a seer, Abd-ru-shin rejects such questions as inquisitive, and gives an answer which indeed is right according to the meaning and corresponds to the truth, but which surely should be much clearer.*

*With my letter I therefore put this question to Abd-ru-shin: Why does Abd-ru-shin reject such questions, which from the human point of view are justified; why does he not openly acknowledge what after all is already known to many?*

ANSWER:

Because I have no need to! Truly called ones will always know it in that hour when they need it, even without my help. But those who think they are called, and yet are not, do not need to know it. Moreover, what is of concern here is *the Word* as such, and not I personally. A mingling of the Word with the person will unfailingly divert part of the attention from the Word to the person. This certainly does not harm the Word, nor the Bringer of this Word, but always him who wishes to absorb the Word undivided and uninfluenced.

He who wishes to hear will hear in any case, and the others would not be helped any more by my being more accommodating. Thus these will at least be saved from perhaps burdening themselves with fresh karma through ill-considered mockery, for which one day they would have to feel bitter remorse.

But with deep earnestness I warn *every* reader and *every* listener *for the last time* also against the pendulum, and advise them henceforth to *turn away completely* from *every* experiment with any of the means employed by the occultists, spiritists, anthroposophists, etc. No matter what it is, it can be the most harmless thing, even the so-called meditations, *from now on everything will be harmful to those who deal with such things!* They will be seized by the Darkness and dragged down without being aware of it, because what is light can no longer come near them.

Every single individual is himself to blame for his spiritual downfall; for henceforth what is light is withdrawn, and a free rein given to the Darkness. It will not hesitate to seize upon those who through such pursuits hold out even one finger-tip to it. With beautiful, hypocritical words, which allow no inkling of the spiritual fall. Whoever did not wish to hear will from now on have to feel; for the beginning of the end has already set in, which every observer who is only to some extent uninfluenced must recognise.

# 38

*What does Abd-ru-shin say about Lorber?*

ANSWER:

I have never read his works, but I know that he was to be a Forerunner for the Bringer of the Truth. Although he personally entered fully into the service of this task, his followers now take great pains to destroy this mission, which in part was joyously fulfilled. He wanted *to lead* seeking men *towards* the Truth-Bringer, but not to be the Truth-Bringer himself. Many of his adherents, however, close their eyes and ears to anything else, and consider what he has brought to be the highest, so that they will even rate the Messages of the Truth-Bringer lower. They thereby undermine Lorber's task and also his intention.

Such a happening, however, is not new, but is found everywhere today, whether it be Baha'i or Anthroposophy, and all other movements small or large, so that it would have been better for many if no Forerunners had come. Fortunately many a coming event will be strong enough to flush away also such dangerous aberrations, and to lay bare the Truth in the process.

However clearly Forerunners have spoken, the adherents in their delusion always seek a wrong interpretation, they stubbornly overlook the clearest hints. They are incurable in their inability to receive something completely unaltered and simple as it is. They always try to give interpretations and explanations in which they can also let their own light be seen! But many a one can yet perhaps be helped through timely recognition in distress. –

# 39

QUESTION:

*Abd-ru-shin does not reject spiritism and occult occurrences in principle, but only the present method of practising them. Is there then some criterion by which one may recognise which of the many circles is pursuing a right course, and which has also reached a certain height?*

ANSWER:

There is, of course, but for the human being always and only up to a very definite degree. Today everything is still too confused, and the false nestles in nearly every circle. Therefore I give no advice in the matter either. But from the first days of the Judgment it is solely *the Word* of the Son of Man and He Himself.

The circles who *recognise* the Word are on the right path, in this world and in the world beyond; there is no distinction here, it applies to all. And the clairvoyants who recognise the Son of Man have *pure* abilities. They will be allowed to see things on and around Him which no one else can have about him, because it is quite impossible to simulate just these sublime signs! And thereby, in this recognition, they cannot ultimately go wrong. But for those who are not pure in heart the ability of clairvoyance is useless and destructive.

Many now think themselves pure in heart who are not in the least so, but live inwardly careless lives in false humility. And at the same time this also brings about a separation among them. The seekers, however, can set their minds at rest – at the last moment of utmost danger and affliction it will be quite impossible to substitute a false Son of Man, because he would not be endowed with the power really to help. He could also bring only human cleverness, but not the Divine Wisdom that is the attribute of the true Son of Man.

# 40

QUESTION:
*What is Abd-ru-shin's attitude towards duelling?*

ANSWER:

A strange question. He who has sought even a little to understand the Divine Laws, which alone are authoritative, will know that any duel is not only childish, because surely there have been enough opportunities to observe that in many cases it was just the more worthy men who fell in them or were physically injured, but that it is absolutely a crime. Not even the most shining cloak can gloss over this fact. The outwardly dignified form of these affairs, which would really be worthy of a better cause, appears downright ridiculous. All those involved burden themselves spiritually, to a greater or lesser extent, with a tremendous guilt, which it will not be easy for them to redeem. In addition they also have to bear and to redeem the effects of all the loss and anguish of soul of those left behind.

It is a sign of striking inner barrenness and emptiness where such abuses of social concepts can develop, which can bring no satisfactory solution to either side, and whose obvious absurdity, coming very near to a childish masquerade, must immediately be clear to any inwardly serious person. But to display manliness and courage also requires *more* than just the outward demeanour of a few hours. *Life on earth* offers quite different opportunities for this, which however just such sham-heroism very often fears and often faint-heartedly flees from.

These are the *duties* towards their *fellow-men*, to say nothing of the inflexible duties towards their Creator. Well, they all have their reward already for such flagrant transgressions, and will also receive it undiminished in the future. –

Views peculiar to society can never alter the Laws of the Universe. He who permits himself to be at the mercy of such views and customs has also buried the genuine core within him, and there is no help for him. By the time he finally awakens from this it will be too late for him. Seen in the true light, a concept of injured honour in the sense of the duel is nothing more than just a part of that self-glorification which would also like to turn the creature into the Creator, which tries to be lord instead of servant. That produces a caricature, like everything which is unsound, unnatural. Thus the fall is, of course, all the deeper.

# 41

★ QUESTION:

*Is the Son of Man already on earth, or is He yet to be born? Why is Abd-ru-shin persistently silent just on this point?*

*Will not Abd-ru-shin give a hint of what is the right course also in this respect to the many human beings who have received His Word with conviction?*

ANSWER:

The near future will bring the answer of itself; for there will be *only one* World Teacher. Nor is the Son of Man yet to be born, but He has been in the midst of mankind for a long time now, as many a religious preacher has already rightly perceived.

For indeed the hard time, during which He will remain as the only One among all the false prophets and leaders who can really bring help in spiritual and earthly afflictions, is *much closer* than even those who are still described as pessimistic visionaries imagine today. Therefore He can no longer be a child, nor is He yet to be born. That would be far too late to bring help in time.

He is just quietly awaiting the time for the fulfilment of His Mission, because today He would certainly be ridiculed, and hated by many circles no less than the Son of God once was.

Why should He acknowledge prematurely Who He is, when the *Will of God* Itself will smooth the ways for Him? He need not join in a race whose goal *is His alone!* None but He will reach it. Who among the really serious seekers can imagine that this Son of Man would now put Himself in line with the many, or even only beside one of those who let themselves be called leaders! Does this not make you smile? He does not court the favour of men, nor will He argue with churches, for He has no need whatever to do so, because this time the Will of God will drive mankind into His arms *as if with scourges!*

*His calm waiting is the most terrible thing that can happen to mankind!*

However, they do not deserve otherwise. They will receive what they have prepared for themselves. Therefore you too should wait patiently until the time is fulfilled.

# 42

*Abd-ru-shin states that the Grail Legend is a prophecy. That I can well understand. But his Grail Message depicts the Son of Man, Parsifal, as severe even to harshness, whereas in the Grail Legend it speaks of the "Pure Simpleton": "Knowing through compassion!"*

ANSWER:

In just severity alone lies furthering love! Moreover, you misunderstand the words: "Knowing through compassion". That Parsifal is a *fighter* probably need not be specially pointed out. Then just think it over quite calmly, objectively: Can anyone really become *personally knowing* through compassion for others? Through what you and possibly many others think of as compassionate sympathy? Reflect deeply, and you will finally come to the conviction that *real knowledge* can *not* arise out of sympathy. Therefore this interpretation is wrong.

Now take it from the other side, and then you will arrive at how it must be interpreted and understood, how it was meant from the beginning. It means: "Knowing through *suffering with others!*" That is more correct. Compassion is really suffering with others! Not merely sympathising with others in their suffering, but actually *suffering* oneself among the others, *with* them. Having to feel everything *through one's own experiencing!* That is something quite different.

Despite divergences from the actual inspiration through the collaboration of the poet's human brain in the rendering, it is still clearly enough expressed in the legend or prophecy that the promised Parsifal must *live through* all the earthly errors in *personal* struggle, in order to suffer under them like many others. Only through this will He finally become really *knowing* about what is wrong in them, and where, when His actual Mission begins, He then has to intervene by bringing help and change!

It is not difficult to understand that as the *"Pure Simpleton"* He suffers everything in the *spiritual* respect through His initial non-understanding of earthly opinions, because He automatically directs His thinking, and with it also His actions, mainly in accordance with the right standard *in the beyond;* something which, in the course of the thousands of years gone by, has become incomprehensible to this mankind and so is absolutely bound to conflict with their opinions, because He came from an entirely different world that lives according to *Divine* Primordial Laws, which in many respects are fundamentally different from the laws that the spiritually erring human beings have devised for themselves here on earth. Hence it is just as natural that thereby He will become severe, and finally at the hour of His Mission will quite relentlessly bend and change all that is earthly, in accordance with the Divine Laws.

*For that purpose,* He Who comes from the lofty distances, where the confused views of solely self-created earthly suffering must remain incomprehensible, had first to *suffer* everything *in Himself* among these human beings in order to obtain the right understanding for it. Without personal experiencing, there cannot arise *that* knowledge which is really capable of bringing relief with a sharp, firm stroke, quite resolute and unflinching. Then the day will come when no twisting and no turning is of any avail to human cleverness. It has been recognised by Him in all its faultiness. The diseased parts will be cut open and removed in order to make the time of their earth-lives easier for aspiring mankind, even making it similar to Paradise.

This task demands the highest knowledge, closely allied beforehand with the earthly experience, in the midst of these excrescences of the human intellect. And therefore the sacrifice of a previous suffering-with-others is unavoidable, if genuine knowledge is to be attained! It imparts the necessary conclusion that severity has to be applied to the point of harshness, since His own experience will always stand before Him as an example.

A natural happening, whose greatness mankind, as ever, will only be able to recognise much later, and with it also the certainty in the spiritual guidance, which always uses all ways only from out of naturalness. In the case of such a great happening the accompanying earthly events, which as secondary effects bring joy or sorrow, hardly come into consideration. Thus it always remains self-evident to the One fulfilling His Task. He does not ask for human understanding or sympathy in it, and only registers every experience with keen observation in His intuitive perception, knowing that it is to serve His training.

And in the end all will be gloriously carried out! The suffering itself, the hostilities through mankind of such various forms, sharpen the sword, harden even the steel of the hammer which one day is to shatter them retroactively in their erring presumption! Looking back after the happening upon the Wisdom of its Creator, the human spirit, filled with humility, will one day bow down in wonder, and willingly *serving* take its place in the working of His Creation. –

# 43

*If stigmatisations are supposed to be partly karmaic effects, then surely these should only occur among the Jewish people, who crucified Christ at that time.*

ANSWER:

Many a reader will be astonished that I should answer such a naïve question publicly. However, I consider it necessary to do so, since unfortunately such a narrow view is widely held.

Reincarnations do not depend on adherence to some religion, but solely on the maturity of the spirit, as well as on the characteristics that cling to it, which it has therefore acquired, or which it bears with it. The degree of maturity, as well as the nature of the characteristics, but not any religious view or creed, release the effect of the attraction-power of the homogeneous species in the world events, thus also with reincarnations.

Therefore many former Christians are incarnated among present-day Jews, as well as very many former Jews among the present-day Christians. Religious barriers are purely earthly, as also is nationality. A happening like reincarnation does not halt before these barriers erected by the human mind, because these barriers or boundaries are not inwardly alive, and are meaningless in world events. In reality these are merely small, insignificant things, which only the little earthman considers important and great, for the sake of ... earthly influence! Nothing more.

A Christian is very often a Jew in his next life on earth, only to be a Christian again later, and vice versa; naturally the same also applies to adherents of other religions. Sex too is immaterial. It changes, or remains as it is, according to the development of the nature of the characteristics or the "propensity".

Apart from all the greatness that lies therein, this circumstance proves that a particular religious view has nothing to do with the real worth or worthlessness of a human spirit, moreover that a religious hatred, as also a national hatred, is something of earthly smallness, base, indeed even laughable because it is absurd. But the concepts of religion can never really come to life in earthman either; for otherwise their influence would certainly have to be stronger and go deeper, remain more lasting! Those few exceptions who are really *alive* in their views, and who therefore also remain more effectively subject to them, so that it will help to influence their reincarnations, cannot be taken as examples.

Therefore it will probably be easily understandable to every reader if I say that the "Living Word of God" can never issue from a particular firmly-established religion either, nor does it ever carry such a religion within it, or wish to! Christ's words about a "church" were not grasped in their great, purely spiritual sense, but unfortunately were made far too earthly, thereby narrowed down and their meaning warped. –

# 44

QUESTION:

*What does Abd-ru-shin say about the various sects and their activity?*

ANSWER:

I will *not* answer questions about various sects, such as for instance the "League of Fighters for Faith and Truth", as well as "The White Lodge" and others; because there is no more time for secondary things, which will remain utterly meaningless for the actual weal and woe of mankind, and for the great events that are to be expected. Attention can only be devoted to *more important* matters, which will then be of help in the gravity of the coming time, and continue to exist as decisive values, among which most of today's endeavours can *not* be counted, for they will not even be able to survive the beginning; because a clean sweep of all that is false will be relentlessly made. To elaborate on this is no longer necessary. All enquirers will find in the World Happening an answer which they do not expect, but which will speak more clearly than words!

If some movements have taken up new thoughts from my Grail Message, and for years have sought to assimilate these in their way as "their own", I would only point out that the first booklets of my lectures were already published in the year *1923*. That will explain many a thing to you. Let us allow these people their pleasure; for in the end it will not endure.

In the Message "In the Light of Truth" I have laid

down what mankind needs. Whether they accept or reject it will be only to their advantage or disadvantage.

# 45

QUESTION:
*Is Buddha an Envoy of God?*

ANSWER:

No. He was no Envoy, not even a Created Being, but simply a developed being. However, he succeeded in turning his back upon erring mankind, and not making himself a slave of the intellect like the others. He tore himself away from that, and because of this he was able, in the actual development of his spirit, to follow the normal and for mankind the really intended way. The earthly intellect could no longer constrict him within its strong, gross materially-bound limitations. In his development he could thus come to the threshold of the Spiritual Realm.

It was only a quite natural consequence that then other people in their limitations regarded him as something apart, something higher. His knowledge, arising from his continued normal development, *was* indeed *bound* to make noticeable a tremendous difference between himself and his fellow-men. –

Thus Buddha followed the *normal* course of the human being on earth. But to rate his teaching, the rendering of his knowledge, higher than the Message of the Divine Envoy, Jesus of Nazareth, even only to set it beside this Message, is simply a sign of absolute ignorance, a clear expression of the generally-prevailing woeful limitation of the ability to comprehend, from which indeed all mankind suffers, and from which just Buddha forcibly tore himself at that time by turning away from it, in order to choose the normal course of spiritual development which Creation clearly indicated to him. But as usual his example is not grasped by his followers in *that* sense in which he gave it, and as he wished it, but is turned into the reverse.

Nor is there any point in saying anything more about it. The very fact that even those who have had the opportunity to become acquainted with the Message of the Son of God nevertheless turn to Buddhism is deplorable enough, clearly marking the inability of such human spirits to comprehend and proving that they do not understand the Message of God, and are therefore also incapable of absorbing my explanations and hints.

It is naturally prerequisite that the sublime Wisdom in its simplicity must be *"found"* in the Message of God, as indeed the Son of God Himself clearly indicates in the words: *"Seek, and ye shall find!"* Hence it clearly follows that whoever is unable to seek earnestly will *not* find.

But it can be clearly recognised that it has not been possible for the European adherents of Buddha's teaching to seek aright in the Word of God's Envoy, because His Message comes from a Height from which one can only receive with a very special and truly humble attitude. It is also understandable that they pass over something they do not comprehend with a smile. It is therefore again characteristic of the restricted state of *their* spirits that they can only seek and find in what is proclaimed by a developed one, who stands far lower than an Envoy of God!

They can only find values in what is lower, because

this comes nearer to their limitation. They lack the potential to comprehend what is higher. Therefore no arguing and explaining is of any use with them; for they could never grasp it in any case.

The movement in Buddha's teaching is from below upwards, and has its narrower definite limit. In the Message of an Envoy of God, however, the movement is from above downwards, and *unlimited!* Hence it is unfamiliar to the human spirit. He must make a greater effort to be able to understand. Buddha's teaching is therefore not a Message, but consists only of recognitions! It is the same with Mohammed. Both followed the right course as Forerunners for the Light. But their words were wrongly interpreted by their followers, and passed on accordingly.

This also indicates quite naturally the spiritual level of the followers concerned, of their potential to comprehend, so limited through their restriction. Added to this there is a certain fanaticism, which is also the sure sign of only a limited part-knowledge. And just this fanaticism in turn still further narrows the horizon of the spiritual ability to receive, often even obscuring everything else, and producing grotesque effects.

Whoever observes all this calmly, and goes back to the root of it, must come to these conclusions already himself. He will then always find as the starting-point either spiritual limitation and the related inability to comprehend, let us say the inability truly to seek; or in contrast to it spiritual freedom, which has an increasing ability to receive and to ascend, unhampered by mankind's sin of intellectual domination.

By these two foundation-stones he can then easily

examine and recognise the wrong or the right way of upbuilding. Naturally the main thing here is that he also knows how to apply the probe *aright*, quite objectively, impersonally, without prejudice.

# 46

QUESTION:

*What is Abd-ru-shin's attitude towards the invocation of saints, does he consider this to be wrong?*

ANSWER:

Invocation is certainly not worship! Therefore the invoking of spiritual helpers and guides is in itself a beautiful custom, if it is done in the *right* sense. There are now very many people who know they have a spiritual guidance. But these spiritual guides, at least those who stand nearest and closest to earthmen, can by no means be called "saints".

It is certainly fitting for the human spirit to render heartfelt thanks to his guides; for they often have trouble and sorrow enough with their charges, much more so than joy. A word of thanks is always appropriate for this thorny activity of guidance. Also an occasional request for help is not wrong, so long as people do not thereby fall into worship, which is due to God alone.

The *highest* guidance-will for every human being lies in the Spiritual Realm. A whole chain of active helpers proceeds downwards from there. But the last of these helpers is always of such a nature that he stands only a little higher than his charge, otherwise he could not come into perceptible contact with him. It is mostly such a human spirit as is still in touch with the earth; for if he were already too high he could no longer be "perceived" by earthman. Moreover, such a guide can still intuitively sense more deeply with earthman, with all his emotions, and can also more readily understand him in them. And when his charge prays, in serious things, the guide will unite with him in prayer, and his intercession has more power for earthly suffering than the intercession of a higher spirit who can no longer perceive the earthly suffering so strongly, because he has lost all understanding for it.

Only *intuitive perception* is the decisive force in prayer, not words, which die away weakly like sound in the wind. Words merely serve us as a help for the soul to become absorbed in the intuitive perception, in order to clarify and to support the direction of the intuitive perception. –

The highest guide-will therefore lies in the Spiritual Realm, and communicates itself to this chain of all the helpers, until the lowest helper, who is nearest to earth-man, seeks to make this volition clear to his charge by making use of all the good qualities and weaknesses the latter possesses, and which only the guide nearest to him can know, through observing and intuitively perceiving with him. It must not be forgotten here that the volition of the guided *human being* is always decisive, because he remains responsible for his actions. The guidance is thus only a help!

The activity of the entire chain of guides then, to the highest guide in the Spiritual Sphere, deserves the gratitude of men for the help given, even though all guides gain reciprocally for themselves through their loyal efforts in guidance. Likewise requests for faithful support can and should be addressed to them by earthman. This is not wrong, but holds much blessing. –

But who can be addressed as "holy"? Only what

stands in *direct* relationship with the Divine is "Holy", nothing else. Therefore we speak of the "Holy Spirit", to differentiate from the Spiritual. Nobody can *become* holy who is not already so from the beginning, because being holy is in turn related to the *nature*, and is not a merit! Unfortunately the word "holy" is often used quite wrongly. Probably no human being who is serious in his reflections, his thoughts and intuitive perceptions can be convinced that sanctification can issue from earth-men, that the opinion or conviction of earthmen plays any part in it at all!

I do not wish to find fault here with the customs introduced in some circles, if they are practised in really good faith; but surely with all such customs there must now and then be a little pondering over things by those who practise them, so that they know *what* they are actually doing. For he who does not know exactly what he is doing can never really benefit from his actions, because in that case they remain just an empty form, a routine, which lacks real life. And without life no prayer can ever rise to the place which brings fulfilment.

Any man who really thinks, however, and does not shirk doing so out of indolence or cowardice, will eventually have come to some clarification within himself. But the thoughtless and superficial would not come to an understanding and comprehension even through the most exhaustive explanation. Whoever has read my Grail Message *aright* already bears the answer to these questions clarified within himself, without my having to refer to it specially. –

But I wish to give yet one more piece of assistance, by referring to reincarnations. This, however, is taken rather prematurely. Only a few will already be sufficiently advanced not to feel the picture that I unroll very strange. I could not really be at all annoyed about this, because the necessary leap from the previously-held views to these facts is, after all, rather great. The inner strength, whose ability to expand depends on the particular maturity of the soul, can with the greatest exertion hardly reach as far as is necessary for this recognition. For that reason too I only wish to reveal one corner of the actual happening, at the risk of its appearing grotesque.

But it would be a great blessing for all mankind, and would facilitate the understanding of many things, if for once they could obtain a clear view *just in these matters*. At first it certainly has an extremely sobering effect, as the Truth always has, but at the same time also a refreshing one. The whole outlook, and with it the earth-life of many human beings, would thereby be immediately and completely transformed to a healthy upward striding. It simply could not fail to make an impression if a human being were able all of a sudden to look about him *properly*, and see that the majority of all those about whom he has learned from the past, through history, many a great, beautiful and also unpleasant thing, are living again with him on earth, in flesh and blood like himself, only now in a different guise. In fact that perhaps he himself is even one of those whom in some way or other he admires or ... has had to despise.

But all that has its time. What he must still smile about today, he will in quite a short time consider to be right and even self-evident. Therefore I say explicitly: With this short reference I am already going a little too far today.

If, for example, I now say that Schiller in his "Wallenstein" describes his own experience, that he had already been on earth before as Wallenstein, and also further back in different guise, this may well require a long soul-activity before becoming familiar with such facts!

And when I say further that, for instance, the famous painter Raphael and also Titian are among those living today, who have no idea of the former happening and of their ability at that time, this will probably affect many a person in a strange way. Only to think that a Raphael in his present guise stands admiringly before a painting which he himself created in his former earth-life. Considering the limitation of the memory, this has even a comical, a humorous effect.

And yet it is neither fairy-tale nor fantasy. Also when I say that Therese Neumann was once the thief on the cross who reviled Christ, and *for that reason* even today still has to bear these stigmata retroactively until inward recognition of this comes to her for the redemption of her guilt, then if not all yet very many, probably most people will doubt this and regard it as fantasy. And yet it will not be much longer till the Truth in this *must be* recognised!

Let us now assume that even Christ's disciples, who according to His own statements did not receive their Master or His Message aright at that time, have been back on earth in various guises repeatedly since then, and that even today most of them are once more among men, what conclusion must a thinking person reach in the course of this reflection, especially if he also gradually recognises the causes and effects concerning these returns?

With this many a picture of the past will collapse into nothingness, and open a view to the joyful awakening of a new, great era of the upward-striving human spirit, who will burst so many old, useless fetters, and stand securely with a free gaze in the Creation of his God, at last serving Him in it knowingly, and thus first and foremost also ... himself! –

# 47

QUESTION:

*Will Abd-ru-shin not also explain how the various designations of other teachings, like those of the Indian teachings, or the occultists, spiritists, and so forth, compare with his designations, such as ethereal matter and others? Certainly it would enable many a person to grasp the right concept more readily.*

ANSWER:

This will *not* happen! The Grail Message stands *living* by Itself! Whoever wishes to grasp It must first of all leave behind him *everything* of the past, without exception. Only thus will he learn to understand aright. And *then* he himself will be able to survey everything so clearly that from the Grail Message he can also illumine what has prevailed hitherto, whereby he will see what is genuine, and what has been contrived additionally by the human mind.

Therefore he must first be born anew inwardly, in order to be able to absorb the new Message unburdened by old concepts. This is the only way open. Thereby what was false will drop away from all the old, and only all that is genuine will remain. Every attempt at comparison must founder on the vitality of the Word of this Grail Message, which is stronger than that which exists now, dimmed by the human mind. But the Grail Message is absolutely one with *that* Word which the Son of God, Jesus of Nazareth, brought.

# 48

QUESTION:

*Is the Grail Message also meant for Jews?*

ANSWER:

The Message is meant, as was once the Message of Christ, for *all human spirits* who open themselves to It! In this sense there are no barriers. Whosoever has opened himself aright is of equal value with all others. Only the actual strength of this opening brings about a difference.

At that time Christ's Message was also addressed only *in the first place,* but not exclusively, to the Jews, because according to the prevailing spiritual development they bore within them the greatest potential of being able to grasp It. Reciprocally, therefore, the Son of God could be incarnated nowhere else (Lecture: "Father, forgive them, for they know not what they do!"). In spite of this the Message was meant for all mankind. The Jews were to spread the Message of God to other peoples who were coming to maturity.

It was by no means the intention to cultivate an absolute Judaism. Nor did one who opened himself to the Truth at that time necessarily have to become a Jew to enable him to enter the Luminous Realm of the Spirit, the Kingdom of God; for only he who *serves* the *Truth* can enter the Kingdom of Light! Religion as such plays no part in this! It is the same again today with all who now wish to open themselves to the Truth.

The new Message of God through the Son of Man,

which has become necessary owing to the manifold distortions of the Message of God by men's sophistry, turns this time, because of the unswerving reciprocal action, to all human beings regardless of nation and religion in whom there is the wish for what is sublime and pure; for the Message of God is once more intended for all mankind in this world and in the beyond, and is to be spread abroad, as was once the Message of the Son of God among the Jews.

Nevertheless, redemption and liberation from the yoke with which they burdened themselves through their failure at that time can now, by this same means, also come for the Jews. But if they let it slip again this time, it will be gone for ever. Never again will they be given the opportunity for it.

Soon, however, great things will also come to pass among the Jews, as among the whole of mankind!

Neither Christianity nor Judaism as such counts for a Message out of the Truth, and thus also before God!

The true Message of God knows only human spirits who are more or less developed, thus more or less receptive. And *that* alone is decisive in the reciprocal action which controls in Creation. And this reciprocal action is a part of the great Will of God Itself, so that actually it is *this* Will that controls in Creation through the absolute reciprocal action, bringing reward or punishment to the originators according to their deserts.

# 49

QUESTION:

*It is said: "But when the Son of Man shall come to judge...". Is the Son of Man appointed as Judge?*

ANSWER:

God alone may judge! The Son of Man brings His "Word" once more. *And in the Word then lies the Judgment!* According to how a man receives the Word this time, so will he judge himself. Through the Grace of God every single individual has once more the free choice. Albeit for the *last time*. As a person stands towards It, either rejecting or accepting, so *is* he then judged through himself, because thereby separation also sets in immediately. To wait is to reject; for to go on waiting patiently is impossible. Impossible also to turn back from the chosen road. This time it is either ... or! And instantly! Hesitation, criticism, and wanting-to-know-better are at an end.

Whatever is not in full and absolute harmony with the new "Word" will fall! To drag over anything that exists is quite impossible so long as one tiny particle created by human cleverness, and not in accord with the Message, is attached to it. The "Word" must now be received absolutely untouched, unchanged and undistorted. There are *no* "agreements" with other concepts! Just as little any "discussion"; for the Word *"is"*!

If man dares to place himself with one leap on the *new ground* without taking with him anything of the old, that is if he trustingly accepts the new Word as the new basis for his thinking and intuitive perceiving, uninfluenced by the old, then from his new standpoint he will quickly see opening up *all roads* which had hitherto been obscure or closed to him, and he will then also recognise where he had gone wrong in the past.

He cannot find the Truth in the new Word in any other way than by first placing himself unconditionally on Its new soil! *He cannot enter from outside.* Too many entanglements hold him back there; he will find no connection.

Effort, self-conquest, and courage are naturally needed for this necessary leap. He who is incapable of that will never reach an understanding. Hence it automatically follows that only those who are *strong in themselves* will arrive at the goal! Those who *are capable* of taking this leap. Everything that is old must be left behind; for what is *right* from all the old is in any case contained in the new "Word", because this comes directly from the Truth.

As a result of this necessary leap, those who are negligent, indifferent and weak in spirit are already eliminated from the outset! They will never reach the longed-for, necessary *"New Land"* which is promised to the seekers, and which *alone* can offer salvation, as the firm ground which never sways and falls.

The "Living Word" can never be examined through sectarianism or dogma! Indeed the reverse: *The Living Word will now form the infallible keen touchstone for all that exists!* And *in this* lies the inexorable Judgment which finally separates the roads of all.

Whole hosts of human spirits who today imagine themselves to be believers, who in false humility would proudly approach God's Throne, will be crumbled into dust and vanish before they can come to the Steps of the Throne! They *imagine* themselves to be righteous, and pay no heed to the Word, they probably even smile about It in their superficiality and narrowness, not suspecting that in It they face the Judgment Sword of the spirit!

Therefore now open the ears of your spirit! You will hear many a thing of value for yourselves, and will not still wait heedlessly for things which are already about to pass you by! – Awake, before it is too late!

# 50

QUESTION:
*What is Truth?*

ANSWER:

Truth is the Eternal-Unchangeable! Which never changes in its form, but is as it has been from eternity and ever will remain, as it is now. Which therefore can never be subjected to any development either, because it has been perfect from the beginning. Truth is *real*, it is *"being"!* Only being is true Life. The entire Universe is "supported" by this Truth! –

Therefore only that which issues from the Truth is really *living;* everything else is subject to transformation through death. For this reason only that which issues from the Truth will alone continue to exist, and all else will perish. Finally nothing will remain in existence but the Word of the Lord, Which issues from the Light and from the Truth, and can only be brought by Envoys of God, Who Themselves stand in the Light and the Truth, Who are thus really living within Themselves! No human spirit, no spirit in the beyond, is in the position to do this. There is absolutely no possibility for it to do so. For this reason those things thought out by the human mind and recognised by the human spirit can never bear real life within them. They remain theories and recognitions, which lack the power of the Living Truth.

"To awaken to life through the Word" means: To awaken to the recognition of the Truth! As a sleeping person can be awakened to the day, so one who is spiritually dead is awakened to the recognition of the Truth through the Living Word. However, just as he who has been awakened from sleep to the day can never become the day itself, so also the one awakened from spiritual death to the Living Truth will not himself at the same time become Life! He will only have his eyes opened for the recognition of this Life. He can never himself become Life or Truth, but only journey on their paths! *He becomes one raised from the dead.*

Here too, also this Word of Christ is to be applied: "Let the dead bury their dead!" That means: Let the many people who would be leaders and teachers go on teaching those who absolutely want to listen to them, and who thus systematically close themselves to the Living Word. Let these dead leaders with their dead words quietly bury their dead listeners for ever, and therewith exclude them from the possibility of an awakening. But *you* who are seriously seeking, *do not* listen to these!

This applies not only to the many sects and societies, but also to the false dogmas of all the great religions. At present no congregation follows the actual *true* path. Neither zeal nor enthusiasm will help to put right the signposts which, through human cleverness, have often been quite wrongly placed on the right path. Whoever trusts in them will never reach the goal, even with the best inner abilities.

Every one who *genuinely exerts* himself for it will discover the meaning of what has thereby been said. However, it requires deep reflection, selfless searching. Such is not for those who think they already know, or for superficiality!

# 51

*Creation had a beginning. How was it before this beginning? Was God then without radiation, without activity?*

ANSWER:

Does this question help you in any way towards your own spiritual ascent? No! Besides, this is something *outside* Creation to which, owing to the nature of the human spirit, the latter's ability to comprehend does not extend. As a creature, his limit is given to him. He must always remain *within Creation,* and strive to recognise *It* aright! Then he will have quite enough to do. And if through this he has finally reached the Realm of the Spirit, in his ascent he has also lost the desire to know things the understanding of which is beyond his comprehension. Only then will he intuitively sense in reverential worship the nearness of the Almighty, Powerful God!

So do not trouble about that. The more perfect you become in spirit, the more discerning you will also become about yourself. With this the conceit of the narrow-mindedness which mainly rules the human spirit today will gradually fall away. You will become ever more humble in face of the Greatness of God, Which comes more and more to your recognition.

The human spirit may rejoice that thereby he will also forget his present grotesque attitude, otherwise he would have to be ashamed of it for ever. Looking back, he would appear ridiculous to himself in his present conceit. From this really childish conceit, arising out of ignorance, also stems the attempt of the so-called clever ones to represent the Son of God, Jesus of Nazareth, absolutely as a human spirit who *developed upwards* out of mankind. They even feel themselves great in acknowledging that He is said to have been a specially gifted, outstanding human being, who rose to the height of a prophet.

These clever ones are really so naïve that the natural thought does not occur to them that even One Who comes out of Divinity to earth must await the maturing of this to Him unfamiliar body, and that He is equally compelled to learn first how to use this earthly instrument aright, before He can begin His task. Therefore He must also first be able to make His brain work properly, all of which as we know requires a certain time, especially as such an Envoy cannot be classed among the mediums – who in their working often unconsciously go beyond the state of their own spirit – nor can He be counted among the inspired ones, among whom are numbered many great artists. But an Envoy from God works *consciously*, out of Himself, because He bears the Source *within Himself*.

Therein also lies a great difference in what is necessary for earthly development, and with it also the solution to the lack of comprehension among some people with regard to the life and work of the Divine Envoy.

And yet again, clearly recognisable in it lies only the enormous megalomania of the incomplete human spirit, who plumes himself on bearing within him qualities capable of development even up to the Highest, thus that he belongs to the Highest of all that exists!

Under no circumstances will he admit that something exists which has *not* developed from below upwards *but comes from above,* from a height which man is not only never able to reach, but not even able to comprehend. Therein lies the so reprehensible and despicable conceit of the human spirit, who flatly refuses to consider such possibilities seriously because it cannot become intelligible to him.

But it does not occur to him to find in it the natural proof that this is simply a height which he lacks the ability to comprehend!

*So small is he in spirit!*

In your question, too, lies a certain smallness, because according to it you suppose Creation now to be *everything* outside of God. How far away you thus are from comprehending the actual Greatness of God!

The Creation to which the human spirit belongs is again, despite its tremendous extent as Creation, only one of the works of the Living Will of God. As a work likewise limited. In the infinity, which cannot be grasped by the human spirit, it appears only like a speck of dust, not more than a star in this Creation!

Besides *this* Creation to which the human spirits belong, there swing yet other Creations, no less tremendous and of quite different kinds. The story of Creation known to the human spirit, but in part not yet rightly understood either, refers only to the development of this *one* Creation entirely by itself, of which men at the sight of the countless stars can divine only the smallest part. The story does not refer to the outworkings of the great Will of God overall!

And this Creation which is known to you is indeed

rounded off as a whole in itself, but in turn contributes in its own qualities only a small part to the *great* harmony of Creation wherein it forms an individual link with a definite task, out of which, however, a sickness like the present failure of the human spirit makes itself disturbingly felt in the All-Harmony. Therefore order must henceforth be restored, even at the cost of cutting off such a diseased link if there is no alternative.

Try to think yourself into this, and you will achieve nothing more than having to clutch your whirling head.

It is better for man now to learn at last to concentrate above all on himself, and on all that is contained in *that* Creation in which he finds himself, to which he belongs, which alone can and shall benefit him for his development. Then he will gradually become perfect as a *human spirit,* whereby will also cease the wish to be anything other than what at best he can become ... a useful human spirit!

As such, every question of this nature will fall away for him, because he will finally recognise himself at last! And this will bring the humility which he so greatly lacks today.

# 52

QUESTION:

*Abd-ru-shin demands that every person should examine the Word. But is everyone capable of criticism?*

ANSWER:

It sounds strange indeed, but unfortunately it is a fact that the majority of men do not in the least know what it means when I say that the Word should be keenly "examined" by every one, so that he may live according to It out of inner conviction.

*To examine is not to criticise*, but it is something that is much harder for man: *to follow with the intuitive perception!* And in this lies the first obstacle.

Man no longer knows how to follow intuitively without prejudice, but approaches every subject with his own little bit of wisdom in order to judge all else by it. Almost every single individual makes this mistake. For the most part however it is societies, and above all newspapers, who sin in this respect, under the delusion that whenever a member or a reader asks they *must* say something, although very often they have no time to go into a question seriously.

If their own little bit of knowledge does not suffice for this, as is only natural in face of the Living Word, then they simply mock and ridicule It, in a more or less "would-be-clever" way, partly really convinced in their narrow-mindedness and partly to conceal their own inability thereby. Whoever is indolent enough to place any value on such earthly wisdom, whoever is guided or lets himself be disturbed by it, becomes a victim of this indolence, which is fatal to him, misses the moment when salvation touched him, and is lost.

But in the beyond such victims will cling like a burden to those who carelessly spread such harm through their "bright ideas", which they only too gladly allow to shine illuminatingly; so that only when *all* the victims have found their way to the height can they begin an ascent, not before! Every seeker can easily explain to himself what this means.

Again many will fail through this obstacle of indolence, of listening to others, of seeking others' opinion first, just as they will through the obstacle of an inability to examine *aright*.

The *right* examination that I have so often demanded requires from the outset the exerting of *one's own* abilities, *one's own* strength! And at the same time, closely linked with it in the reciprocal action is ... the awakening of every single one for himself. Thus the blessing of making the effort follows immediately. But this can never happen if someone takes the opinion of others as a basis for himself.

Each one must do the examining, that is, the earnest following with the intuitive perception, *by himself alone,* quite quietly in his inner being. He must *listen within* himself, must hear whether kindred sounds for this are heard there, contrary to a previously held opinion!

A call from God goes out directly to each individual human spirit, because each one for himself alone must also bear the responsibility for all that he thinks and does! That is what makes it impossible for societies to form where a Word of Truth is concerned, because each

142

one must strive to deal with himself in this! He cannot lean on others or seek their counsel.

Whoever shows such a lack of independence is from the outset already lost for *a life of his own*. He need not even trouble himself, for in any case he will never reach the final goal. Whether he is lost now immediately, or only later, is of no great consequence for him! It would be wrong to leave such spiritually indolent people with unnecessary hopes, which will not be fulfilled anyway.

It is better for anyone who cannot follow the Grail Message spiritually to continue heedlessly on his way, rather than wanting to display his clever ideas about It; for the hour will unfailingly come when *too late* he would still like to think better of it; then, however, his present childish arrogance will form a millstone that holds him down. –

The Grail Message grips all human beings at their weakest point: their self-conceit nourished over thousands of years! Hence so much touchiness, often mocking smiles, still more indulgence in apparent superiority, out of which all too plainly speaks the deepest anger, and yet all of which in the end only bears direct witness to what the Grail Message says of mankind. In all the twisting, wriggling, turning, mocking, inveighing, hatred and would-be cleverness they show the thinking observer, as in the clearest mirror, everything they refuse to acknowledge and seek to attack as existing facts! But the struggle is utterly in vain! A pity that so much energy should be summoned up for it; for this Truth holds fast quite relentlessly and is victorious. Resisting and wriggling will avail men nothing this time.

They only paralyse themselves thereby; and in the

ensuing exhaustion they will perish within, or else they must condescend to turn back on to the right course. Already now it is firmly established in many souls, for their salvation, even though for the time being it makes itself felt only in disquiet, until one day the bright flame of sacred recognition breaks through the dross that today still lies over it, fulfilling its purpose in spite of the opposition by developing even to the greatest force all the strength of the spark smouldering beneath it, through the heavy resistance. Thus even the evil must henceforth become useful to the good. –

All who can no longer perceive God's call within them will be turned away from the gate of the Spiritual Realm whenever they would desire entry later on. They must go back into darkness and horror! They may then seek in vain for counsel and help from those whose words they blindly trusted, only so that they would not have to exert themselves spiritually, as well as out of fear of any kind of responsibility. They can no longer be helped; for through this they lack spiritual "life". They belong to the dead who will no more awaken.

How could they enter God's Kingdom when they have closed themselves to hearing the call, and preferred instead to cling to the comfort of religious dogmas, which do not require the trouble of *personal* spiritual activity and the *awakening* demanded by God! Not everyone is capable of such self-conquest, for it requires the *whole* strength that a human being is capable of exerting, and above all a more humble recognition of himself! –

# 53

QUESTION:

*I have had the opportunity in various towns of seeing how the Grail Message is studied by readers who have united in circles. I was struck by the diversity prevalent in them. Whereas in one circle many trends were discussed, and then compared with the Grail Message, the speaker of another circle took only the Grail Message as a basis, and allowed nothing else to be considered. Now, which of the two leaders is the better qualified to help mankind?*

ANSWER:

There are those called by the Light and those chosen by men, or such as feel themselves to be called. There is a great difference in the effect. The one called by the Light serves God, and therefore knows only the Will of God, Which from the beginning was, is, and will remain unchangeable, and therefore permits of no concessions whatever, offers no possibility at all for deviations, and hence appears to be severe. He cannot allow anything to be discussed other than the Will of God, Which cannot be distorted.

But the one chosen by men, or who feels himself to be called, in the first place serves men, and therefore makes concessions to them. If he is serious he will try gradually to guide their wishes into a single wish, in order to bring them to that point where they will finally wish only to honour the Will of God, through which they will become capable of also understanding aright the one called by the Light. They will then no longer perceive any severity in his teachings, but will recognise the straight road.

Where there is only one road, people *must* naturally follow it if they wish to reach the goal. It is wrong to say that many roads lead to the Light. *Only a single one* leads there, which lies in unconditional fulfilment of the Divine Will. There is no other. And since the Divine Will is *quite definitely* given, there are no compromises with the wishes of men either. What is different for man is only *the way in which he follows* this one road, what he uses to help him in doing so, which depends on his developed personal abilities. But these different ways of following it do not alter the road, much less its direction.

It is also wrong to maintain that the one who serves men thereby also serves God. As is well known, a person can serve only *one* master. But on the other hand, the Called One who serves God always helps men at the same time. It goes without saying that this help cannot always coincide with men's wishes, because true help rarely lies in the fulfilment of wishes.

Those who serve men are naturally more acceptable to them, because they are more convenient for them. But they are by far the weaker ones. Most of them will always become the victims of their followers.

# 54

QUESTION:
*What is Grail Service?*

ANSWER:

Grail Service is fulfilment of the *Divine* Will, without consideration of the will and the desires of men. –

The concept of "Grail Service" must not be arbitrarily extended. An adherent of the Grail Message does not at the same time stand in Grail Service; for he simply draws practical applications from the Message for himself in order to find and tread the path to the Light. Through this he comes to the Kingdom of God, without as it were being able to speak of a Grail Service.

Grail Service itself demands much more. True, the way to it is open to many human spirits, but only to a few is it finally given really to attain this goal. Even for the human spirits who already dwell in the Spiritual Realm, the Grail Castle is still so far removed as to be beyond earthly imagination. Even to grasp *aright* the "giving up of oneself" is a step which many human spirits believe they have indeed taken, but … this exists only in their imagination. The giving up of oneself is by no means dissolution of the self, or passing into a dreamlike Nirvana according to Oriental thought; but it is the strongest fully self-conscious activity that can be imagined – the highest degree of *personal* activity. Something quite, quite different from what the easy-going human spirits imagine. This state goes far beyond the present human conception. One can just about assume the direct opposite of all that has so far been thought about it, in order to hit upon what is right. Readers however should content themselves with finding the way to the Light and being able to ascend. This is already the longed-for bliss, the highest towards which the really good person can strive. It is the crown of human life.

# 55

QUESTION:

*Is anthroposophy following the right path? Many of its adherents want to argue about the Grail Message.*

ANSWER:

The adherents of every sect are convinced of its truth, and especially of their own wisdom. They read and listen to everything else only in this one-sided conviction, thus they no longer seek, and therefore cannot find anything either. Through this they have become blind and deaf. They would look upon even the clearest truth as nothing but an intentional animosity, and reject it as soon as it did not correspond to their own knowledge.

Therefore I am glad that I have no need to answer such questions as yours, because already now we have entered upon *that* time in which every man will soon personally *experience* whether he has followed the right road or whether he only imagines he has, and whence *alone* help can come to him. In *this* way, and not through words, will the false prophets be exposed and topple. Hence remain calmly watchful for just this short span of time. *Soon* you yourself will find an unmistakable verdict. On anthroposophy as well.

Therefore simply let people squabble about the Grail Message. In blind rage many a zealot even wants to find contradictions in the Message just where the most logical objectivity is most clearly apparent. But if a serious reader goes to the root of such contradictions as opponents assert, he will soon see that these assertions of contradictions have been only a reflection of the particular attacker's inability to understand, or testimony of how stubborn he has become in the absurdities of his own opinion, which in defiant obduracy he is not prepared to give up. Thus on scrutiny the attacks merely reveal themselves as evidence of the spiritual poverty of those who wish to let their wisdom shine forth through them. In most cases these people have not read the *whole* of the Message at all, but after only a fleeting glance at individual parts simply give tongue, as an expression of fear and anxiety that their hitherto-imagined greatness might suffer through one who knows better.

Some even go so far in this absurdity as seeking to maintain that the Message contains nothing new at all. Well, this does not even need a reply. I think that this very assertion already bears within it the right judgment on those concerned, showing that they completely lack any possibility of comprehension, and that with their power of absorption they simply cannot cope with the actual contents of the Message. These people should quietly go on adhering to more easy-going associations.

But no attack, no scorn, no mockery will avail them ... they will all be buried under the ruins of their false would-be knowledge, and fortunately for them they will soon be forgotten, while the Message will endure.

# 56

QUESTION:

*Will Abd-ru-shin not reply to the various expressions of hostility? As an enquirer I happen to know personally that in many things it would be easy for him to turn back the spears that are directed against him.*

ANSWER:

My Word is too precious for me to waste it on such things. Nor have I any need to do so, because the answers to this will come from an entirely different direction. Be quite calm; nothing will remain unanswered, not even the smallest thing. In a way which will probably serve as a lasting lesson to all humanity. I need add nothing to it.

And as for the many "views" and opinions, or even the announcements which you enclosed for me by so-called racial experts and graphologists who would detect just in me a pure-bred Jew, these could probably give no better evidence of their incompetence in their "knowledge" than exactly that; for there are not many families reaching far back who are more thoroughly German, and more so-called Christian, than the one from which I come. But that would not have been of the slightest importance to me, who know only *human beings,* and do not judge by races, nations or religions. That is too petty, and unworthy of the true human being. Do these people believe that they may one day enter the Kingdom of God with national colours and anthems? No, such narrow-mindedness cannot induce me to reply.

But it has also become the fashion in certain circles simply to try without scruple to represent many a thing that might endanger their own wishes or ideas as a pro-Jewish effort, in order to keep many people from occupying themselves with it, and in order through cheap self-protection not to lose ground, but rather to be able to further their own ends by not exactly laudable means.

Besides, how one-sided these racialists are who attempt to judge merely by outward things, by gross matter, whereas the actual man *is the spirit,* which *alone is decisive.* And this spirit is older than the present and the former physical body. Just let us consider it in the purely earthly sense: A good man will always be the same, even when he changes his clothing repeatedly. In his everyday attire he is exactly the same as he is in his Sunday clothes. It is no different with the spirit, the actual man.

I am disgusted when I reflect upon these absurdities. And on what is all this pride, all this arrogance founded, which so many assume towards the Jews, among whom there are human beings whose hands one would much rather clasp in a friendly way than those of one's fellow-Christians? After all, what is Christianity based on? Only upon Judaism! Christianity can record only Jewish Prophets of the Old Testament, not others. The Ten Commandments came only through a Jew. The Disciples were Jews.

The future will bring many a thing concerning which the scoffers of today will have to be ashamed of their present opinions and their present knowledge. Many an hour will come for them when they will wish they had been silent, instead of puffing themselves up in their wretched conceit. It is foretold that everything must become new! So many are looking forward to this fulfilment. But is there a more dreadful condemnation than this very promise? Does not there lie in it the fact that everything, everything is wrong, if everything is to become new, that is different, in order to be right at last? And in this time we are now standing! Of all the things that men have devised and created for themselves, there is really nothing left that is not fundamentally wrong. A greater proof of this than the present decline and the present hopeless confusion is surely not needed.

## 57

QUESTION:

*I try to live according to the Grail Message. Often, however, unpleasant thoughts, which I do not at all want, crowd in on me. Often I even want the opposite. But then the unpleasant thoughts crowd in all the more, and absolutely drum in my ears. I have to suffer much from this; for it troubles me, and I am inclined to despair over the question of how it all comes about, and whether perhaps I am inwardly evil.*

ANSWER:

You yourself write that every time you merely *think* differently from how you wish to. Therefore your inner being must be better than your temporary thoughts. Surely you will also always *act* according to your *volition*, not according to the nature of your thoughts. Besides, there are only a few people who fare any differently. You need not be alarmed about it. Such thoughts, with which one's own volition is not in accord, have little power. The forms produced by them very quickly scatter again, without being able to do any harm. Provided, of course, that you do not continually supply them with fresh strength by too much brooding over them. Pay less attention to these unwanted thoughts, and they will soon stay away of their own accord. Otherwise a short fervent prayer will help.

# 58

QUESTION:

*How is it possible that so many people can find nothing in the Grail Message, while to me, with the Bible, it is everything?*

ANSWER:

These people are probably predominantly sectarians, but not men who are still inwardly free. Whoever says that the Grail Message is easy, or offers nothing new, does not know It, has drawn nothing from It even if he has read It – in short, just he has not grasped It. *It was too difficult for him,* and *therefore* he finds It easy. That really says everything! Such a person, however, can take comfort in the thought that the Message is not meant for him either. He to whom It gives nothing has thereby received just what he deserved. Indeed this is part of the sifting. Later experiences will plainly show it.

# 59

QUESTION:
*Why does God sometimes punish so severely?*

ANSWER:

God does not punish at all! Nor does He threaten and tempt. All these are false human opinions. Even the Ten Commandments, which were given through Moses, are merely a guide to show how man can attain to a life of bliss. Only man inflicts punishment in his social system. Like everything thought out by him, but unfortunately in the wrong way, imperfect, and still more imperfect in practice. The word punishment has really only been invented by man himself in his limited comprehension.

Let us take an example of a rather mundane nature, so that it is easier to understand: A businessman has gone into partnership with another. One of his friends is more farsighted than he, and has a better knowledge of human nature. Consulted by the businessman because of various business difficulties, this friend warns him, and advises him to dissolve the partnership as quickly as possible, as the partner harbours evil intentions, and wants to pursue his own advantage relentlessly to the disadvantage of the businessman. The friend told the businessman concisely and clearly that he would suffer great losses unless he followed his advice. The businessman, however, did *not* follow this advice, as he could not then detect any signs of the truth of his friend's misgivings.

Not until some years later were the warnings of this friend fulfilled. The businessman suffered great losses through his partner, who had been able most cunningly to carry out a plan well laid beforehand to the detriment of the other. The businessman now called it a punishment for disregarding the warnings of his friend, and sought to interpret this punishment as a chastisement for it.

*Such* is the attitude of men towards the Light. From there many timely warnings are sent to them, through observing which they can save themselves from many an evil. Now, however, they imagine that it is a punishment of God when they are struck by the self-incurred evil, which had to take effect through their refusal to listen or their disobedience. They even think themselves marvellously great when they bear this "punishment" with patience, and expect a special reward for it from God, be it only in the sensation of inner upliftment through their good behaviour.

All this is self-deception and falsehood; for God does not punish them thereby, but they in their obstinacy have created the misfortune for themselves. It can be observed from the Light when a man, or all mankind, takes a wrong path, which must inevitably lead to a very definite end. This end, which man sometimes cannot see, or better still does not want to see, is clearly recognised from the Light. Man or mankind are warned. When the warning is disregarded, and men stubbornly continue on their way, it is natural that at a certain time they must come to this end. This end however is not brought about as a punishment by the Light, but was already prepared through men's choice of the way; and the Light had only tried to hold men back from it, to lead them on to another course, where the evil end was avoided and a joyful end awaited them instead.

Thus God does not punish, but man, if he will not allow himself to be warned, brings about everything himself. Therefore it is great sacrilege to say: "God, how severely Thou dost punish!" and it is also wrong to complain: "How can God allow such things!"

# 60

*What does Abd-ru-shin say to the assertions that spirit and soul dwell side by side in man?*

ANSWER:

Whoever asserts this has no idea of Creation. Spirit is the origin, the core and the final goal of man. Spirit is he himself, without any other kind of covering. Soul is this same spirit enveloped by one or several different coverings, but without the gross material covering, the physical body. Therefore the soul must also bear within it the spirit itself as the actual, living human being. As soon as the spirit has gradually laid aside the ethereal and animistic coverings, whereby it rises ever higher and higher, it finally stands as a human spirit in only a light spiritual covering, and can thus enter the Realm of the Spiritual, Paradise. More detailed explanations about this will come later.

# 61

QUESTION:
*What are slanderers?*

ANSWER:
They are people who cleverly distort facts in order to give them a wrong meaning to the detriment of other persons. Those who invent new stories and spread them abroad for the same purpose are not slanderers but liars. According to the Divine Laws, the one is as reprehensible as the other. They are classed with the attempted or committed moral murders in which the karma is just as severe as with murder committed in the gross material, in most cases even more severe, because injuries to the soul are more lasting, especially since in many cases other persons are suffering as well. Moreover, it is karmaically difficult to redeem *any* attempted or committed moral injury, whether substantiated or not. This should be easily understandable, because such a deed in itself always presupposes an unclean character; for a pure or simply a noble character would not commit it, and out of a healthy abhorrence would completely reject thoughts of that kind. Hence in such things the uncleanness will naturally always be on the side of the perpetrator, who thereby automatically brands himself as such.

# 62

QUESTION:

*Why does Abd-ru-shin refuse to unite with existing associations? In many cases it would certainly be easy to come to an agreement. People ought to join hands in striving upwards, and work together, whereby the high goal would be reached much sooner.*

ANSWER:

I am not here to lead people out of their self-created errors by explaining to them or disputing and arguing with them, but I *bring a Message* to which men can cling in order to extricate themselves from their errors. There is no "agreeing" over this, but only: "either – or!" Nor is there any working together, but at best a following. Whoever is incapable of making that clear to himself should quietly leave the Grail Message alone; for It would benefit him nothing. Whoever does not regard It as a gift from God will never understand It. Nor is It for him. I do not seek to "persuade" a single person. And I have *no* intention of founding an "association" or a community, and living on their annual contributions.

Therefore I remain independent, and would not think of studying all the assertions of men, some of them completely absurd, in order to refute them in laborious argument over and over again. In my opinion this would be doing too much honour to the ridiculous arrogance of so many men.

God reveals the Truth, *as It is* in His Creation. It stands amidst the hopeless and dangerous chaos that mankind have brought about. To recognise and to accept the Truth as such is solely the concern of men, who have to strain every nerve to gain for themselves this most precious treasure, without which they will be irretrievably lost. *Man* must do *everything* for this, because God will not run after him, He will never debase Himself to become a servant of man! But that is what man with his strange attitude has hitherto expected. *He* always demands proofs! But *he* should exert himself to recognise the Truth! After all, it is entirely to *his* own advantage. And he who seeks really earnestly, who therefore makes an *honest* effort for it, *will* find the recognition!

From the very outset, however, *that* humility which recognises one's real self is indispensable for this. And that is just about the most bitter thing for man of the present time. He will already founder on this; for he is not capable of it, *he does not want it!* And therefore he forces on the Judgment. Just look at man, how he struts through earth-life, adorned with all the trumpery of earthly vanity! What place is there for humility?

Finally he even imagines that the conflict of the Light against all Darkness, which has now begun, is taking place solely for his sake! But the great struggle is *not for him* personally. The ascent which is thereby made possible for him is only a consequence of it. If he neglects to use this last opportunity with all his strength, if he refuses to hear the call, then he will remain stuck fast in the self-created quagmire and suffocate. There will be no mourning for him!

Burdened with what the human mind has created, he will never recognise the right way.

But I go on my way alone in the fulfilment of the task

which I have recognised. Indeed, no one need follow me who does not voluntarily declare his willingness to do so. I really think that my language is always plain enough. A compromise, however easy and simple, is with me completely out of the question from any aspect. Connections with societies, sects and churches can never be considered, nor are they known by God; for by Temple of God, Church or Cathedral is meant something different, far greater than some organisation on earth! –

# 63

QUESTION:

*Why does not Abd-ru-shin some time also speak in his lectures about practical earthly things?*

ANSWER:

Men have greater need of what I have said hitherto, as will now shortly become evident. I am not governed by their wishes. I leave that to all those who write "for the sake of profit".

# 64

QUESTION:

*I can say that in my seeking I have examined, as seriously and objectively as is humanly possible, the various fields of occultism, and have eagerly studied theosophy, and later anthroposophy.*

*Everywhere I found beautiful and true, furthering things, but only the Grail Message through Its clarity, and above all Its simple conclusions, brought me the crown. The good that I had found in all the others I found all over again in the Grail Message. Hitherto I had received everywhere only disconnected piecework, but now I saw something complete, clearly arranged in understandable sequence, which gave me a clear picture, and only through that the certainty of my knowledge. All the hitherto separate parts have become one living whole, through the right connections and the filling-in of the hitherto-existing gaps.*

*I have spoken of this with theosophists and anthroposophists whom I had known from earlier times, but none of them had any wish to understand me. Despite the many new things which had never before been uttered by anyone, they saw nothing new in the Grail Message. They felt the simple clarity to be inferior. What can be done about it?*

*After all, people must realise that they cannot accomplish much with individual parts, however good they may be; and that only he who shows us how they are put together, and thereby reveals their full application, as it is in the Grail Message, must be the Master. Not since the pure Teaching of Christ have I found again such clarity and depth.*

ANSWER:

Why do you still need a reply? You give it to yourself in the very question. Calmly leave these people to go their own way. The Message is not for them! Moreover, the Grail Message has not been put together, but It is by Itself alone, completely separate, independent. I have already spoken about this a number of times.

Nor are you alone with your letter; for several others of a like nature have arrived, even with similar wording. Your experiences only confirm that to be understood the Message demands greater earnestness and diligence than superficial people think, and that It always speaks solely and directly to the *individual soul* alone, giving it *just what it needs for itself* in order to ascend.

Through this vitality, which follows no set pattern, It is naturally bound to break asunder any sect and thus becomes a great danger to its existence, because the Message forms independent people, *free in themselves*, who must be opposed to all sectarianism. It is a foreboding instinct of self-preservation when organisations, societies and sects oppose the Message by ignoring, mocking or disparaging It, or by showing hostility to It.

The Message, however, "is" and "remains" when all else falls apart, and will allow nothing to hold It up on Its way, which every attack *must* even further.

# 65

*What is serious seeking?*

ANSWER:

It is precisely *not* all that which is designated as such today! He who seriously and therefore *honestly* seeks the Truth must first cleanse himself completely within. That is to say, he must empty himself of all that he has so far learned and read, putting it completely aside, as well as shutting out every person; and then he must intuitively experience the "Word" quietly within himself, like a child standing before something new. Not for nothing does man often find in children the most unerring judgment of things and people, because they face everything impartially and innocently.

It sounds easy, but it is actually the hardest thing for the man of today. There is no greater obstacle for him than just this. And since I demand *serious* seeking *as the basic condition* for being able to absorb the intrinsic contents of the Grail Message, I therewith make on man the greatest demand that can ever be made on him. Thus I also simultaneously and quite definitely exclude from the outset all those who pride themselves on their own knowledge. A sifting, by which only the humble can receive the palm of true recognition in logical reciprocal action, while the others leave empty-handed.

To recognise all this *intellectually* will be reserved, with a few exceptions, solely for the *new generation* which will survive the present time; for only the purified intellect, which has been *forcibly* cleansed of all the dross of the present errors and vanities through experiencing, will bring the uninfluenced potentiality necessary to grasp it!

This *new generation,* however, is not to be expected only in centuries to come, but is already living, and will become new only because those of various ages who belong to it will emerge *purified* from the wheels and stones of the mills that even now are beginning to grind! While all others will be crushed in them.

Such a serious seeker will not look for alliances, he will not join any sects, nor feel the urge to unite with others. He will inwardly digest everything by himself, since no one else is able to help him to do so. Only *in this way* will it become alive within him, and be his possession, which he cannot share with others. –

# 66

QUESTION:

*I have what is perhaps a rather strange question, but I hope to receive a reply because so many people speak of it, and as I have been able to observe, they very often torment themselves with it and are oppressed by it: What really is an inferiority complex?*

ANSWER:

Because this question is of general interest it shall be answered here. An inferiority complex, as it is so pleasantly called, occurs where the spirit cannot unfold freely. In many cases it is even proof that such a person is spiritually stronger than he is able to manifest, and for that reason he suffers from the pressure of a restraint which he cannot account for. Read my lecture "The Mystery of the Blood". You can glean many a thing from it with regard to this very question.

But there is yet another cause, for which there is little help: that is, indolence of the spirit! Man could indeed pull himself together to throw off this pressure if only he wanted to do so. But he is too lazy for this, and would like others to do it. Besides, as time goes on, he actually feels quite happy in his display, and he would miss something if the pressure were to leave him. He wants to be pitied; while he asks for advice and help in many quarters, he would not be particularly grateful to anyone who could really free him from the accustomed pressure.

The first kind can certainly be helped, but not the second, because they themselves do not really want it.

# 67

QUESTION:

*Every time I have seen and heard the opera "Parsifal",
I have been left with an uncertainty regarding the conception of "the Pure Simpleton" ("der reine Tor"). If only
I had absolute clarity about it, the impression would
probably be much stronger still.*

*(The German word "Tor" has two distinct meanings.
One signifies a "gate", the other means "simpleton". In
English, therefore, two separate words must be used.)*

ANSWER:

In my lectures on the Primordial Spiritual Planes I
have already spoken about this too.

In any *deep* thinker the figure depicted as "the Pure
Simpleton" ("der reine Tor") must arouse an uncertainty. This uncertainty arises because the expression, as
well as the whole portrayal of the figure, is an error, for
which I have given the reason in my lectures.

It would lead too far in this reply, therefore I shall
content myself with indicating that Parsifal is "the Pure
Gate" ("*das* reine Tor"), but not "the pure simpleton"
("*der* reine Tor"). Everything lies in this, and the knowledge of it, together with a different conception, will set
your mind at rest. In reality Parsifal is the Mediator to
Creation, therefore also to humanity, and is the Gate of
Truth and of Life for all Creations downwards.

# 68

QUESTION:

*I have often read in newspapers of people with X-ray eyes. I have never been able to arrive at a clear under-standing of the process, nor have I had the opportunity to hear anything more definite about it; but I can imagine that a person who really has such a faculty will have a much finer perception than any manufactured instru-ment. Is it possible to have a detailed explanation of this?*

ANSWER:

The fact that such abilities exist is already widely known through the newspapers, nor is it any longer disputed, because it cannot very well be denied. Doc-tors, too, have already interested themselves in it in order to fathom this apparently still mysterious pheno-menon, and then to use it to help mankind.

The investigations, however, have not yet gained a sufficiently firm footing to be considered and used as established knowledge. Nor can this firm footing, in the sense hitherto customary to science, ever be created in it either; for these abilities, which in themselves are very rare indeed, are of such different kinds in the individual human beings that they cannot be regarded at all uni-formly.

If you bring together five persons gifted in such a way, you will find that each one of them works in an indepen-dent, distinctive manner, "seeing" more or less clearly, and by no means always the same as the others. The particular personality of the gifted one is too great a factor here, just as also his degree of culture forms the mode of expression, and even strongly prejudices the "seeing".

The less such a person has acquired specific knowledge through study, the more uninfluenced, thus the more surely and clearly, will he be able to make use of such a gift; otherwise quite unconsciously the acquired forms of opinion intervene, which then make the actual picture of the illness appear different.

But on the other hand it can happen that a person who is uninfluenced by what he has learned does indeed see the picture of the illness correctly and undistorted, but is unable to express himself so as to render it correctly.

Thus there are disadvantages in both cases, which often prevent an *exact* rendering, and thereby may even bring dangers, if a person gives himself up to such things unthinkingly.

It is best if talent and science work together in this connection, but naturally not in one person. That is to say, if a doctor stands by a person thus gifted, whose descriptions of the picture of the illness he learns in time to understand exactly, and then adds his knowledge and experiences in carrying out relief.

In this way a very beneficial activity can arise from it. But it is not advisable to depend unquestioningly and readily without careful verification on the picture of an illness which has been "seen" through a talent.

Here too, as everywhere, there are naturally exceptions, which however are very rare. These exceptions of particularly strong abilities might be called not merely gifted, but rather blessed individuals. These persons, however, will never fail to advise consultation with a

172

doctor, who will take into consideration in his work the picture of the illness which has been seen.

It would, of course, also be wrong for a doctor to refuse such unusual help out of some prejudice. But a doctor who is a doctor "from within", and who wishes above all to *help* mankind, will never do this.

Now in addition there is something else:

Such abilities or gifts may appear in men, and after some time simply disappear again! Like so many things, this is closely connected with the alteration of the blood composition; for only a quite specific radiation of the blood induces the "seeing with the eye of the spirit", as the suddenly-appearing gift of X-ray eyes may be called.

So-called X-ray eyes are not the eyes of the physical body, but figuratively speaking they are the eyes of the soul, which must first have paved a way for them *to be able* to see such things. And to serve this purpose there is the radiation of a quite specific kind of blood composition, which can form itself and then one day change again. With it the ability which is so often wondered at simultaneously arises and vanishes. In this also lies the true explanation!

Indeed it is well enough known that even quite famous mediums suddenly lose their outstanding gifts, or that these are weakened, without any reason hitherto being found for it.

Where this happens the blood composition has merely changed in some way, and with it also its radiation. And in the type of blood radiation alone lies *every* medium-istic ability, whose variations in turn come through the various bridges formed by the respective blood radia-tions.

Thus the key to all these things is the blood! It cannot be said, however, that there is only *one* specific blood composition that produces mediumistic gifts, but there simply exists one definite *basic species* with many ramifications, which have the most delicate, at times perhaps barely perceptible differences.

The knowledge of the effects of the blood radiations, and the knowledge of the possibility of a deliberate change in these radiations, will one day become a very special knowledge, but significant for the help of mankind. *In it lies everything earthly for man!* His physical health, and the full unfolding of his spirit on earth. It is the *most important* earthly help that can be given, embracing everything, and bearing within it happiness and peace.

Today the oft-used expression "poisoned blood" can rightly be spoken of, for this is actually the case, only different from what men imagine by it.

The bridge to everything, hence also to the outstanding abilities, is thus the radiation of the blood! I must still point out many paths in this connection, in order to create a complete picture of the tremendous importance of this hitherto unrecognised field of activity, which will now soon open to *those* human beings who, for the sake of helping, strive to fathom what until now have been the secrets of Creation, in order then really to work *servingly* in the new knowledge, but not to make a "name" for themselves by it.

One thing I should like to point out particularly here: With the so-called eye of the soul, in most cases the finer radiation of the illness is recognised, not merely what is physically visible. This latter, which becomes visible to the doctor, thus to the physical eye, plays only a second-ary part there, if it is seen at all. But just this *finer* kind of seeing is the more valuable and important; because it thereby recognises the *seat of a disease,* the actual start-ing-point, which like all else consists of fine radiations, and only calls forth the effects that become visible to the earthly eye.

Therein lies the advantage and the greater importance of making use of such "seeings"; and if to one so blessed it is given in addition to be able to "perceive intuitively" – again seeking connection through the radiation of his blood – what in this or that case can assist recovery, or at least help as an alleviation, then this is a grace which can scarcely be estimated, and can actually work miracles.

However, since most people of today are accustomed always to seek only their advantage, and accordingly regard everything that concerns others in the same light, since many always assume only the worst of their fel-low-men, which really is only an echo of their *own* inner being, and makes it impossible for them to believe in people whose thoughts are idealistic, therefore persons so gifted diffidently draw back, because to them the gift of this ability to help is much too sacred, their volition much too pure, to expose it to defilement.

Yet again, it is not to be assumed either that working of this kind should be given entirely free; for not everyone thus gifted is also at the same time so blessed with riches that he can continually afford to give such help without an equivalent return. Any other views about this are unhealthy, unjust and presumptuous.

But the fact that there are also people who, taking advantage of such highly promising fields, seek to conduct shady transactions in them, thus who do not give right value for payment, or perhaps even none at all, is no reason to discredit what is genuine. Where is there any field of human activity at all in which abuses of this kind do not exist? One would probably look in vain.

From all these motives it is understandable that many a truly gifted person, who could bring great blessing, withholds his abilities and does not make the help available to men.

Yet in this question, even if not directly expressed, there certainly lies also the wish to learn whether it is advisable to make use of such abilities, if the opportunity arises to do so.

If it is received in such a way as I have already explained, it is undoubtedly to be recommended; for it surely gives great reassurance to anyone for once to learn from such a source what state his body is in. In this way many a thing has been found out that it was very necessary to know, and thereby it has been possible to get rid quite easily, even at the start, of many an ailment which later on might have had very harmful effects.

It is here as with many things in human life. Man often passes by opportunities without making use of them for himself, and later when he no longer has them he longs for them. Like an undefined pressure, the thought that he has missed something continues to weigh on him.

# 69

QUESTION:

*I have often pondered where, in the experience of the Son of God Jesus in the wilderness, the actual temptation through the Adversary lies. Yet I have not come to a right understanding. Can Abd-ru-shin throw any light on this?*

ANSWER:

It is good that this question is asked now, for it has never yet been fully discussed. Probably the true meaning of the temptation at that time has never yet been found either because in this too, as in all spiritual matters, man has remained much too superficial. Of course the possibility of a right understanding presupposes the knowledge of my Message. I shall try now to grant a deeper insight:

Jesus went into the wilderness in order in its solitude to further and facilitate the necessary breakthrough of His recognition concerning His own descent from God, which was essential for the fulfilment of His work.

The sensing of the Power connected with this gradually filled Him with a great urge, and sought to take effect, but He was not able then to become fully aware of it. Only a few days more, and also the knowledge of His Power in its gross material effect would have lain before Him in full clarity.

Then, however, it would have been too late for the Tempter, if he wanted to induce Jesus to do something which was bound to harm His work from the outset.

Here too the Tempter, as always, skilfully seized a point in time that was favourable to his intentions. In this case it could only be the time of transition between the intuitive perceiving of the emerging Divine Power and Its conscious application in the Light of Divine Wisdom, which was pressing to break through at the same time.

The Wisdom knows the immutable Laws which the Will of God placed into Creation, out of which Creation first came into being and is also maintained.

The Adversary *knew* the Laws, and built his plan upon them. Most skilfully he chose the moment when Jesus was becoming ever more conscious of His Mission and His Origin, but did not yet have a completely clear recognition, that is, while things were still fermenting and surging within Him. That was the only opportunity and possibility of laying snares which might have lured Him into a rashness that would have been detrimental to His future task, and from the beginning would have rendered His appearance before men ineffective for a long time, or at least greatly weakened it.

Thus he soon found the most vulnerable point for this attack, which lay in the unspeakable Love of the Son of God for men. Jesus did want to go to meet mankind with open arms, and in joyous helpfulness, because He was the Embodiment of the Love of God on earth.

Thus the Tempter flattered: "If Thou be the Son of God, command that these stones be made bread!" The deeper meaning implied in this was that men would then hail Him in order to open themselves willingly to His Word, which He wished to bring them for their salvation through the Knowledge. Thereby Jesus would

178

immediately have won the people for Himself at His first appearance, and His work would have been easier.

Therein lay the temptation! It was indeed an alluring objective for the Love Who wished to help in the Word, Who naturally bore within Him the aspiration to be able to work as quickly and also as effectively as possible.

Now if it could have been done in this way, there would have been no question of a temptation, but everything would have revealed itself as a help towards a swifter accomplishing of the work of the Son of God, which was by no means the intention of the Adversary.

At the root of the temptation was the plan to induce Jesus to do something which was not possible for Him, and through which He would have disillusioned men! But this could only happen at a time when Jesus was not yet "ready for His earthly work", when indeed He had already intuitively perceived within Himself the over-whelming power to work miracles, and had also sensed His Divine Origin, but had not yet struggled through to the recognitions necessary for conscious working. Nor therefore was He yet capable of surveying the self-acting Laws laid down in Creation through the Will of God, into which He could and ... had to place His Power, because these Laws flow out of God the Father through the Divine Will and are perfect, and therefore cannot be distorted.

For this reason Jesus could never have turned the stones into bread, because this is not possible in the Laws of Creation; and just as little could He have cast Himself down from the pinnacle of the temple without injuring His physical body.

Thus the temptation lay in the Adversary's wish to

entice Jesus into doing something which must prove unsuccessful for Him, so that He would thus undermine men's belief in His Mission from the beginning.

The Tempter knew the Laws of Creation, knew the limited thinking of earth-men, which indeed is still widespread today through the delusion that the Perfect God in His Omnipotence would perform arbitrary acts, which are opposed to His own perfect Laws in Creation!

Taking advantage of all this at a time when self-recognition had already matured in Jesus to the point of breaking through, when it was urgently moving in Him but not yet lying clearly before Him, the Adversary sought through his promptings to deal even in advance a heavy blow to the work of the Son of God, or to make it altogether impossible, choosing as suitable soil for this the then still impetuous Love and the urge to help, and spurring them on even more. *Therein* lay for Jesus in His development the temptation, which was aimed at violently disturbing the whole Work of Help before it had even begun.

But stimulated just through this, the *knowledge* in the Son of God also broke through at the same moment, and He repulsed the Tempter.

Now it is really strange that various Christian-religious denominations regard it as the highest belief to see the Perfection of God, as well as His Omnipotence, *in this*: that He can simply do *everything* without adhering to His own Laws of Creation, in which His Omnipotence lies, thus also readily to assume that Jesus as the Son of God could have made bread out of stones.

But just through designating and also acknowledging this demand of the Adversary as a *"temptation"*, they themselves really prove the rightness of my explanation of the Laws of Creation in my Message! For if their belief that Jesus as the Son of God could have done this was right, the Adversary's suggestion would not have been a "*temptation*" but actually a great *help*.

A temptation, however, is always meant to bring harm, as indeed was also the intention of the Adversary. Thus in admitting that this happening was a temptation, and at the same time teaching the unconditional belief in miracles, there lies a contradiction which cannot be bridged, and which clearly shows that true knowledge is completely lacking in these teachings, and that they are treated with boundless superficiality.

Thus the gaps in what religious institutions have hitherto taught are revealed in thousands of things, and even at a cursory investigation automatically bring to light much unsupported ignorance.

# 70

*Is there a "Providence", or has the teaching about it arisen merely out of the endeavour to smooth the path through earth-life for faint-hearted human beings?*

ANSWER:

Providence is nothing other than reciprocal action, on whose clearly-marked courses stand helpers to assist *those* human beings who follow their courses aright. Therein also lies the predestination of an earthly path. Providence is actually the *after-effect* of earlier decisions in experiencing! But the man who short-sightedly wishes to believe in only *one* earth-life, for this reason calls these after-effects, which are in accordance with the Laws of Creation, Providence; but by this he really means only the influence of the helpers who stand on these paths ready to help those of a good volition, for which reason a "kind Providence" is very often spoken of.

Thus it is by no means wrong to use the word "Providence", so long as people do not form a wrong picture of it. Actually, however, the so-called Providence is only a part of the real thing.

# 71

QUESTION:

*How did the expulsion from Paradise actually take place?*

ANSWER:

Before answering this I must ask a question in return: Does the question refer to the course of the natural development of Creation, or to what took place in connection with the "Fall of Man"? For these are two entirely different things, which have no connection whatsoever.

For the sake of simplicity I will answer *both*. Let us first take the course of the development of Creation. Here it is a question of the departure of the unconscious human spirit-germs from the boundary of the so-called Paradise, in order to be able to return there fully conscious.

This is a completely natural process, which is actually better described by the term "expulsion". The expression "throwing off" renders it still more clearly.

During the coming-into-existence of Creation in its continuous development, it is the departure of the unconscious spirit-germs, their detaching themselves from the sphere of the spiritual precipitation that adjoins Paradise through the urge to become conscious, thus the beginning of their journeying through the Worlds of Matter for the purpose of developing consciousness.

That is not a punishment, however, but a Grace. And this I have already explained in greater detail in my Message, as pertaining to the Knowledge of Creation.

But the punishment that followed the *Fall of Man* was an independent process, which again like everything else also took place quite naturally, and affected already-developed human spirits.

The Fall of Man took place on earth, and has to do with the awakening of the intellect, which awakening was to have been given to man through Lucifer to raise him in the World of Matter. But not so that man should bow down before this intellect by regarding it as the highest. He wanted to rule through it, and thereby enslaved himself to it, instead of making it into a keen-edged instrument for his journey through the Worlds of Matter, in order lovingly to ennoble and uplift all that is gross material in gratitude to the Creator.

Since the intellect is *earth-bound,* and will always remain so, the human spirit bound itself through it, and cut off every connection with the Luminous Heights, its actual homeland.

He deprived himself of the connection with the Light so necessary for him, thereby cutting himself off from a return to the homeland. As soon as earthman himself put the intellect in the highest place, he was like a sack tied at the top, because he thereby blocked his view upwards.

For the intellect, as a product of the earthly brain, can understand only all that like itself belongs to gross matter, issues from or is closely connected with it.

It therefore naturally rejects what cannot be classed with this gross matter, or else faces these things "devoid of understanding", which means the same as being unable to acknowledge them.

This choking-off from all that is higher, and not of matter, is equivalent to being cut off from Paradise, which will surely be easily understandable to every thinking person. When this took place man was on earth, and not in Paradise, from which he cut himself off.

Even the saying: "In the sweat of thy brow shalt thou eat bread" is not difficult to understand in this connection. These words were not actually uttered; for it was not necessary, since the natural consequence thus followed automatically.

As soon as man, through the domination of the intellect, had cut himself off from Paradise, which lies in the Spiritual Sphere, and from all that is higher and beyond matter, because he could no longer understand it and therefore could no longer have any knowledge of it either, all his thoughts and actions, in accordance with the intellect, *had* to be directed only towards all that is earth-bound. Through this arose the striving *towards only those things that are in themselves low!* Thus the gaze of earthman turned away from above, towards the earth and all earthly requirements, for which he exhausted all his strength. Therefore in the end he could do nothing other than struggle for his daily bread, in the sweat of his brow and in contest with his fellow-men.

Therein lay the punishment, which however resulted automatically from the turning away from God and His Luminous Heights to the World of Gross Matter, from which man had laboriously to wrest the things he desired.

This happening, in itself automatic and matter-of-course, was figuratively rendered in the Fall of Man and the expulsion, which was nothing other than a cutting-off from the Paradise of the Spiritual.

185

The temptation took place not in Paradise, but *on earth*; for the serpent could never have entered Paradise, quite apart from the fact that the spirits who live in Paradise could not have been tempted in this way at all, because they swing and work only in the *intuitive perception*. There they have no need of the intellect, which belongs only to matter, and at which the temptation was aimed.

# 72

QUESTION:

*Surely it often happens that through external circumstances a person is thrown off the course which he had set himself to follow. He has to accept either a position or some work that is not in harmony with his true goal, whereby he loses much time which he must regard as being unprofitable to him. If in addition performing the work even costs him an effort, without bringing him any pleasure, it surely cannot benefit his spiritual maturing.*

ANSWER:

Loyal fulfilment of duties always brings spiritual gain. This gain is naturally vitalised and heightened if one's heart is also in the work. But often such occupations are necessary bridges, which the person concerned still needs to enable him to reach a higher goal, which will then fill him completely and thereby also become a joy to him.

So obviously with such transitional occupations, which may sometimes last many years, there cannot always be satisfaction and joy, least of all if the person needs this work for his own development and for his spiritual advancement!

Very often he sees much later that the very years which he considered wasted, and in which he imagined himself to be off his really intended course, were for him the most important ones, which he would not have missed on his earthly path at any price, because he urgently needed the experiences of them for the attainment of a higher goal.

Then he will give thanks with his whole soul for the wise guidance that apparently pushed him aside.

# 73

QUESTION:

*What is to be understood by the term group-soul? I have often read this designation in various books, but have never found a real explanation of it that could give a true picture of the conception.*

ANSWER:

With this question a point has certainly been raised which it would require a whole series of lectures to clarify, and which naturally cannot be accommodated in a simple question-and-answer form.

Nevertheless I will at least define this matter in broad outline. It is best if I at once interweave it with another question that has been put forward, and which reads thus:

"As well as human beings, do animals, plants, etc., also have souls which go through a process of development; and what happens to them when they depart this life?"

To this it has to be said that there is nothing in Creation which can remain without development; for the Law of Movement does not permit of this. Thus the souls of animals, originating from a special species of the Animistic Ring which is the first to surround the Worlds of Matter, also develop.

Here I cannot do other than refer for once to my lectures on the different Rings or Planes of Creation, because knowledge of them is absolutely necessary for an understanding of this answer, and a more closely defined picture cannot be given, since everything in these planes is and remains in motion.

Thus the souls of animals, which issue from the lowest Ring of the Animistic Sphere, and which are not of a spiritual nature, develop ever more and more on earth. Hence they are also subject to corresponding changes.

On departing from this earth these souls in the initial stages return to a group-centre, or better said they are attracted by it, whereby they again lose their form and enter this centre. There is not just *one* group-centre; but centres exist for every degree of maturity. Here too, in obedience to the Law of Homogeneous Species, everything unites in gradations of the particular maturity.

But with higher development of the animal souls, the form of the soul remains in existence after an earthly death for a period which lasts ever longer, and it can then also incarnate again without having merged with a group-centre.

In this connection devotion, loyalty or love is the binding force, which holds the form together in the longing.

The conception "group-soul" comprises species of lower animistic substance from which the animal souls sever themselves, to return there again after gross material death, because they are attracted by the gathering-points. According to human earthly conceptions it is a formless mass, from which parts taking on form sever themselves as souls, and on returning lose their form and merge with it again.

In reality, however, these group-souls consist of many indistinct formations, intermingling, interlacing and constantly changing.

190

I explain it in this way only in order to give an approximate concept of it, because to enter more closely into it necessitates the reading of my lectures.

Just one thing more should be mentioned here: Only those creatures such as animals, which are able to move about, through which they have the possibility of being able to protect themselves, possess the souls just mentioned.

Plants and rocks, however, do not possess a soul of their own, but only form dwellings for elemental creatures, such as elves, etc., who can move out of them at will, without experiencing direct pain if their dwellings are damaged.

These elemental creatures care for and tend the dwellings given over to them, which cannot move from their place of their own accord, they build on them, and feed them through radiations, which then appears to human eyes like an independent life of these plants.

# 74

QUESTION:

*For a long time now I have always tried to do only my best, and yet I have to experience again and again that I make one mistake after another. One could almost despair, and must assume that a spiritual maturing here on earth is not possible at all.*

ANSWER:

It is better to make mistakes with good volition than to do nothing for fear of making mistakes! In most cases a person who makes mistakes advances in spite of them, if he draws lessons from them for the future, so that he does not always repeat them. His spirit will certainly mature at the same time if his volition is good, and if he does not deliberately intend evil.

# 75

*How is it that so many people are unable to recognise the Working of God in Creation, but live as though God did not exist?*

ANSWER:

Because such people do not open themselves! But if a man cannot see any higher working in Creation, it must be due to a quite considerable accumulation of obtuseness. Such a condition, however, is not inability of the human spirit, but solely superficiality or indolence! Certainly they eat and drink, and think of gaining earthly advantages, but not for a moment do they ask themselves whence comes the origin of the beautiful Creation to which they themselves belong, and its maintenance. They take and enjoy, without wishing to seek the Dispenser.

Such people count even less before the Creator than animals, because they have the advantage over the animals that they bear within them the possibility of recognising, and they are simply too lazy to make use of this special ability. This may seem sharp and severe, but it corresponds to the facts. In reality they are idlers, the drones in Creation, even if they are considered industrious and important among earthmen.

193

# 76

*What is the difference manifested by a human soul which leaves its body at a natural death or a violent one?*

ANSWER:

The soul that passes on through sudden death is like a fruit that falls from the tree *before* it is ripe, and still has to ripen afterwards. This soul that has come over too soon must in some way, in accordance with its nature, make up what it missed on earth.

But even a death that men call natural may be premature for the soul, if the earthman has neglected his physical body or paid too little attention to it, that is, if he has not sufficiently cared for it as property entrusted to him, or has even harmed it. This can very easily happen through too much drinking or smoking, and also through other propensities or habits that are not in accord with the healthy needs of the body.

Who among the human beings knows by how many years an earth-life is often shortened through some stupid and apparently harmless habit, to say nothing of the passions, or ambitious excesses in sports.

Through all these customs and bad habits, probably the souls of one-half of the "cultured" earthmen of today have to leave the body for the so-called beyond too soon, and thus could not fulfil their time, if they had thought at all in the right way of a fulfilment and a higher purpose of life on earth.

# 77

QUESTION:
*What is Grace, and how is it related to Justice?*

ANSWER:

In the human sense Grace is an arbitrary act, but not in the Divine sense. God's Grace lies in the self-acting Laws of Creation that bear the Will of God, Which at the same time is also Justice. In their Justice they give the fallen human spirits the possibility of achieving ascent again through redemption.

These effects of the self-acting Laws of God in Creation bear within them Justice and Love, and at the same time are also the Grace that God offers to human beings.

# 78

QUESTION:

*I know the story of the Incas, the "Children of the Sun". They were good-natured, and yet through the ill-famed Pizarro they met with such a terrible end. Was there such a heavy karma clinging to these people that in view of their purity and childlikeness they could not have redeemed it symbolically? Considering their harmless lives, how is the terrible catastrophe that overtook them to be explained?*

ANSWER:

Very simply! Through the harmless way in which the Incas lived they would have come to a standstill! They were quite happy in this state, and had no urge to develop further of their own accord.

They lived like innocent lambs. But there were other people on earth besides, who had already succumbed to the disastrous influence of the domination of the intellect, and thus resembled wolves. As is well known, however, lambs and wolves cannot live together.

Moreover, the enquirer must be clear on the point that not all misfortune can be due to an *existing* karma; for even the karma must surely at one time have had a beginning.

Any reader of my Message knows that even today, in addition to the existing karma, not only are karmaic threads severed every hour, but also *new ones* are always being knotted.

Thus these malevolent men who suddenly attacked the

196

Incas knotted a new karma, whereas the Incas benefited in spite of the earthly affliction; for they *awakened* in order to go on developing in the spiritual *and* earthly sense!

From this event humanity can learn once more that it is men's duty to be always *awake*. Spiritually *and* in the earthly sense. However high man on earth stands spiritually, however good a life he leads in the Light, if he is not at the same time awake also in the earthly sense, if he forgets his earthly environment, in which after all he has to live as an earthly human being, if he will not heed it but will live here on earth *only* for his spirit, he will and must suffer harm, because he then gives a free hand to his ill-disposed fellow-men. Thus he allows the weaknesses and faults of his fellow-men to increase, and even provides them with the opportunity to give vent to them. That is wrong!

In the Message I have also pointed out explicitly that on earth what is earthly must go hand in hand with what is spiritual.

To be awake is the best defence, and the hardest struggle!

*That* is important for every man on earth.

Through wakefulness much evil can already be turned aside before it even comes to the point of attack. *That* is the *right* struggle, as it is demanded in the sense of the Will of God. *So* should all fight: In and through unceasing *wakefulness!*

## 79

QUESTION:

*It has struck me that especially against Abd-ru-shin ever again fresh attacks are attempted with great venom. The nature of these must really have a repulsive effect upon cultured and thinking people. I have not only experienced this with various sects, but have now had to observe it even with the churches.*

*This gives me much to think about, for such behaviour really shows the reverse of an exemplary life in the Christian sense, as should be expected and demanded of all people who directly belong to and serve in a church, if the genuineness of their words and doctrines is to be believed in.*

*By no means does it accord with the intention of the Son of God Jesus, upon which after all the Christian churches are based; that much is certain for any Christian who is in earnest about his Christianity. How is it possible for such things to happen, which by their nature must indeed rock the whole foundation? Or am I in some way wrong in thinking this?*

ANSWER:

Surely the answer already lies clearly enough in this question. It is quite logically thought out, and needs no further explanations. Throughout world history it has always manifestly been only the representatives of the religions dominant at the time who have fought against Truth-seekers and Light-Bringers, as soon as these went beyond the bounds of the given religious precepts in order to draw closer to the Truth.

No one can contradict these world-historical proofs; and indeed the Son of God Jesus Himself did not fare differently, that is common knowledge. If He were to return today, exactly the same would again happen to Him, only adapted to present conditions. Even clergymen have more than once preached this from the pulpit in all honesty, and probably no person who knows men and their behaviour will expect anything else.

But the *nature* of such attacks, whether these take place secretly or openly, can always mark only the particular persons from whom they emanate, who indeed remain responsible before the Laws of God, which in any case must automatically take effect against them in the end. The manner in which it is done is characteristic only of the *persons* concerned, and impresses a corresponding stamp upon them. The enquirer, however, should not charge the churches themselves as a whole with it.

# 80

*A question already answered leads me to put another one: It should surely be easy for Abd-ru-shin to throw light on all the weak points and faults of the churches or sects, through which their attacks would probably cease out of prudence.*

ANSWER:

Does the enquirer expect me to pursue in this matter the usual shady and reprehensible methods that are so characteristic of the opponents? I could certainly do this, and it would fill volumes; my task however lies not in this, but in showing the way to those men who earnestly seek God and Truth, thereby helpfully offering them what they seek.

That also explains many a question with regard to why I do not strive to find readers and adherents through the usual publicity, and to expand their circles rapidly.

I offer to the seekers, but I do not solicit. He who truly seeks *will* find! He will find because it is so willed by God, and helping forces from the Luminous Heights lead every serious seeker to it. These same forces thereby also help me, and at the right hour mankind will have to experience that I stand in God's sacred protection. With that, the falseness of all the attacks will automatically be exposed, and the end will be *such* that these very attacks and all similar actions will have contributed the most to *furthering* my Mission, in spite of their contrary intentions.

It lies in God's Law that at this time the Darkness with its evil intentions must now also, against its will, serve the Light.

My own knowledge, in implicit faith in my Mission and its outcome, gives me the right, even with regard to the people who ask, to remain silent in answer to the attacks, and to leave men to decide for themselves whether they wish to believe these animosities. All they need do here is to think of the words of the Son of God Jesus:

"By their *works* ye shall know them." That is the same as: "*By the nature of their activities you shall know them!*"

Surely the recognition of the true nature of the opponents is then no longer so difficult?

Besides, with such attempts at suppression and persecutions a grave sin is committed directly against one of God's principal Laws: Man is to have his free resolution in his decisions, which is something that cannot be separated from his responsibility; for where there is responsibility there *must* also be the free ability to make resolutions! But that ceases where the freedom to examine and to weigh is cut off by authorities who, as can be clearly enough seen, only seek thereby to maintain their own influence.

Where there is really Truth, light can be safely thrown upon it, there is nothing to fear, and indeed there would be the least reason to inveigh against that which is different or new. On the contrary, anything different can only strengthen the Truth.

It is man's most sacred duty to move *forward* in the recognition of God, as well as in his spiritual development. Any hindrance in this, and any shackling to what exists, is standstill, which brings about retrogression.

Scientific investigation and discovery through the intellect always advances steadily; if spiritual investigation does not keep pace with it, it must in time be shaken violently and begin to waver, because the balance necessary for harmony between these two different kinds, which are meant to go hand in hand, is lacking. The end will then be the inevitable collapse, because intellectual science lacks the necessary living spiritual support; for mysticism cannot give this to intellectual knowledge.

These comments apparently do not belong to this question, but only apparently so. In reality they deepen the meaning of the answer, and I hope that many a person will grasp this.

# 81

QUESTION:

*As a serious reader of the Grail Message, "In the Light of Truth", by Abd-ru-shin, I also wish to bring to life within me the lecture on prayer, which is so important.*

*In view of this, I feel that it would certainly be a great blessing for many people if Abd-ru-shin were to give a basic form for prayer in everyday life, which can be adhered to . . .*

ANSWER:

This is not the first suggestion of the kind, and therefore I have already given for the circle of readers the basis of a Morning Prayer, a Grace before Meals, and an Evening Prayer, whose meaning accords with the position of man in Creation. If man exerts himself not merely to "recite" the words given, as most people do, but to concentrate on experiencing them inwardly, that is, swinging with them, then *that* really effective prayer which man is capable of sending forth will arise. My words are intended only to give the outward hold for it, and to sustain the intuitive perception.

The prayers are:

1. *Morning Prayer:*
   "Thine am I, Lord! To Thee alone in gratitude I dedicate my life; O graciously accept this my volition and grant me the help of Thy Power this day! Amen."

2. *Evening Prayer:*
   "O Lord, Who art enthroned above all the Worlds, I beseech Thee: let me rest in Thy Grace this night! Amen."

3. *Grace Before Meals*:

"O Lord, in the weaving of Thy Creation, Thou hast graciously set before us an ever-prepared table; accept this our thanks for Thy Goodness! Amen."

# 82

QUESTION:

*Many Bible-believers cling so much to the "miracles"
of Jesus. How does Abd-ru-shin explain the miracle of
the feeding of five thousand people with a few loaves and
fishes? According to the Laws of Creation it is impossible
to multiply food a thousandfold.*

ANSWER:

This too has been fully explained in the writings which
give an account of Jesus' life on earth. As always, and
even still today, rumours arose among men at that time
which not only distorted the spoken words of Jesus, but
also wove even around His Person vastly exaggerated
stories that lacked any actual foundation.

Jesus Himself was often horrified when He came for
the first time to a place where such rumours had already
preceded Him, which must have made Him despair over
mankind. One of these was also the story of the feeding
of the five thousand people, which did *not* correspond
with the facts. It is true that five thousand people
listened to Him, and during this time He fed them with
the *Word* of God, Which is food and drink to the *spirit,*
but not with earthly things.

I myself have fared no differently during these latter
years. Rumours have been circulated which in view of
the facts are absolutely ludicrous. So much of it could be
described as an insult to mankind, who are expected to
believe such things. Even in the immediate neighbourhood of my home there were newspaper reports of a

castle, sometimes of a citadel, and other things, whereas I live in quite a modest house, as can very easily be verified. There is also talk of happenings which can only originate in brains with morbid tendencies or ... with *deliberate evil intent,* to prevent people from approaching my Message seriously.

In many places the reason for this can naturally be only fear that through coming to know my Word the human spirits will joyfully awaken, and begin to reflect deeply on things whose explanation they find in my Grail Message, "In the Light of Truth", and nowhere else.

It was no different in Jesus' time on earth. Rumours were invented and spread abroad, partly out of fantasy and exaggeration, partly out of malice. If mankind then believed in the stories, and Jesus could not comply with corresponding requests in other places because they did not accord with the Laws of Creation, people were bound to imagine that He simply did not *wish* to! In this way resentment was cunningly disseminated. Unfortunately the false rumours were also retained for later on, and thus came to be handed down.

But surely people only need to be alert and observe their fellow-men *today,* and they will also readily find the explanation of many a contradiction from former times; for men are still exactly the same today as they already were even then.

If a hundred years hence someone reads today's reports of the newspapers from my immediate neighbourhood, it will not be surprising if he fully believes the rumours circulated in them, in the delusion that everything must certainly be true if it was reported in the close vicinity.

# 83

QUESTION:

*Does the one-sided cultivation of man's frontal brain mentioned in the Message also have physical disadvantages, in addition to the terrible spiritual consequences of this hereditary sin?*

ANSWER:

Very many, because the physical body is adapted to the *harmonious* development of the brain, and not to a one-sided one. He who knows the importance of the brain for the human body will readily understand this. Through the wrong treatment very many of the body's abilities, which would otherwise have unfolded to the great benefit of man, remain suppressed; others again can just barely assert themselves, while in general many illnesses which humanity would otherwise have been spared also arise.

All this results in a constant and very considerable shortening of the earthly life-span.

At a later time, after the transformation has taken place, mankind will recognise with horror how much they have also sinned in the earthly sense through this deviation from the Laws of Creation, and what harm has thereby come about. Many illnesses will disappear completely.

It would be pointless to go into these things any *more fully* just now; for the changes will come quite automatically, and in such simplicity, with the absorption of the undistorted Living Word, that the transformed human beings will only shake their heads over the pretended "high knowledge" of the distorted age, whose emptiness had to come to light through itself, and collapse.

# 84

QUESTION:

*It is often so difficult for me to recognise my fellow-men aright, in such a way as would enable me to assess them according to their inner worth. And the disappointments then distress me. Many a man who has achieved really great things turns out on closer acquaintance to be very small in his personal nature. How is this possible?*

ANSWER:

If a man is to be recognised by his inner worth, and not merely by his perhaps great earthly works, attention must be paid to the *little things* that he reveals in his character.

It is just the many unnoticed little things that show the *essential* thing, the personality of a man. It is very seldom that a man stands *in* his *works*, but rather in most cases he places these *before himself*.

Only a *mature* human spirit is *one* with his works.

He alone is thereby also truly *alive* in his daily work, in contrast to the many who merely do their work automatically, but themselves remain *beside* this work.

The latter naturally also lack the real joy of work. It is true that such people can also be loyal in fulfilling a duty, yet they look upon this fulfilment as a compulsion, in the most favourable cases as a compulsion *necessary* to life; but they never find any real satisfaction in it, thereby no joy either, and are always longingly casting furtive glances towards something else.

This something else usually has little to do with *work*,

but rather with the fulfilling of desires for enjoyment, which for the true human being should arise only out of the fulfilment of duties, and of joyfully performed work; for *true* joy and undimmed pleasure arise solely in the consciousness of loyal fulfilment of duty and work joyfully done.

Here, too, observe human beings in the small things; then you can very quickly recognise whether they do their work *wholly*, that is joyfully, or automatically. It is by this that they are to be assessed.

# 85

*Among other things in his Message, Abd-ru-shin
speaks of a great Law of Creation, that only in giving can
there really be right receiving. I should be grateful if I
could have still more precise references on just that point,
which will guide my thinking on to the right course.*

ANSWER:

This Law permeates everything. With a little observation it is not difficult to recognise it and learn from it.

It extends not only to the *conscious* and willed thinking and doing of men, or to their work in various pro-
fessions, but also to all processes which are looked upon
as self-evident, and which to a certain degree take place
automatically.

Let us just consider breathing! Only he who exhales
rightly can and will automatically also carry out healthy
and perfected inhalation. Indeed through right exhalation he is induced and compelled to do so. This gives
health and strength to the body.

In exhaling man *gives!* He gives out something that is
of benefit in Creation, to name here only carbon, which
is needed to nourish the plant. Reciprocally, or as the
after-effect, *that* man who exhales with care is placed in
the position to breathe in again deeply and with pleasure, whereby great strength flows to him, quite differently from what takes place with shallow breathing.

But this is not the case the other way round. Man can
breathe in deeply and enjoyably without thereby being

*automatically* compelled also to exhale thoroughly; for most people carry out exhalation in particular in a superficial way.

They do indeed seek to take with enjoyment, but it does not occur to them that they should also *give* something.

And from the neglecting to *give* aright, that is, to breathe out completely, many things result: Firstly, because of this man can never come to the right enjoyment of breathing in, and secondly, not all that is harmful to or cannot be used by the body, and which must burden it or impede its healthy swinging, is expelled or discarded, as a result of which many kinds of diseased conditions may arise in the course of time. A close observer will recognise also in this the unobtrusively working Law.

It is no different in coarser physical things. The enjoyable intake of food can only be achieved through digestion, thus through converting and passing it on for the nourishment of earth and plants. It is absolutely dependent upon it.

And as it is with physical things, so is it also with spiritual processes. If a spirit wishes to draw, thus to receive, it must pass on transformed what it has received. The transforming or forming before the passing on strengthens and steels the spirit, which in this strengthening becomes capable of receiving ever more and still more valuable things, after it has made room for this through the passing on, be it by word or writing or in some other action.

Only after the passing on is the spirit lightened, otherwise it would be weighed down, would constantly

212

be made uneasy or restless, and might finally even be completely overcome. Only through giving, that is, through passing on, can the spirit in turn receive anew.

I only mention these things, which can be easily observed and understood, in order to indicate thereby what is great and in constant activity. All processes in Creation are subject to this Law. In its outworking it naturally manifests always in a different forming, according to the plane and the species concerned.

This Law can also be differently described, and illumined from another angle, by saying: Whoever receives must pass on, otherwise congestions and disturbances which are harmful and can become destructive will ensue, because it is against the automatically-operating Law of Creation. And there is no creature who does not receive.

# 86

QUESTION:

*The allegation has often reached me from Germany that Abd-ru-shin is a Jew. For years now I have heard of this time and again. It is obviously the intention to cause some harm or other thereby; hence I should be grateful to have a reply to this some time from Abd-ru-shin himself, whose attitude in this matter, as always with all attacks, is one of dignified reserve.*

ANSWER:

I can answer your question with the greatest simplicity: The allegation that I am a Jew is a lie, and a very *clumsy* lie at that, because in this case the opposite can readily be proved, as has not always been so easy with some of the slanders hitherto, which through the distortion of facts have been very cleverly planned.

In this case I have not concerned myself with the actual points of origin, but if everything there rests on such a shaky foundation as this ludicrous and obviously evil-intentioned lie, then in the long run things will not be in a good way with them.

Years ago a German newspaper, with the same intention, even published a picture of me, from which I could recognise that for this purpose a photograph of myself must have been tampered with by retouching, thus falsified, because there was no longer any resemblance to the real photograph. Perhaps the newspaper concerned was misled by it. However I then kept silent as well, because it seemed to me too ridiculous to say even just

214

one word about it.

Whoever wants to believe in such things, and rejects my Works *on that account,* or does not wish to read them, must just do so; for I do not force my lectures on anyone.

Although for me it is an entirely secondary matter, I possess evidence of my so-called pure-Aryan origin dating back to the 16th century. These proofs have been collected by upright and honest-thinking people; it was not done at my instigation.

My Message Itself however is *objective,* and is addressed to *all* men who are permitted to spend a certain time on earth. I should be acting against God's Holy Law if I were to make any outward distinctions in the matter.

# 87

QUESTION:

*Strict church believers often refer to the account in the Bible according to which, at the appearance of the Son of God Jesus, the doubting Thomas was permitted to put his hand into the wound in His side, and also felt it to be such a wound. From this they try to prove that, contrary to the explanations given by Abd-ru-shin, the resurrection must have taken place physically.*

ANSWER:

This is the usual convenient kind of reasoning by church believers, who simply rely for proof on Biblical passages which only in rare cases do they really understand aright, and which hitherto have not always been interpreted in the right sense either.

Besides, a reference to the Biblical report is by no means an actual proof, which will surely be at once evident to any independent thinker.

On His appearance among His disciples Jesus, like any other departed one, at first still wore only the body of finer material substance, and not the gross material one. To enable Thomas to be convinced that it really was Jesus, Thomas was given the grace of being able to see and to feel *ethereally* for this moment, thus to let his own ethereal body function.

When the human spirit is still in the gross material covering, the ethereal body sees and feels *through* the gross material body. This gives the impression that it is the gross material body itself that is acting. At the same

216

time the gross material body very often also makes the appropriate movements in an outwardly visible way, it goes along with it, so to speak.

So it may be also today on quite different occasions that a person gifted with ethereal sight and touch reaches out for something, and also feels as quite natural, what others are unable to see.

It was no different with Thomas. He saw and felt with his ethereal body and its organs, *right through* his gross material body, the already transfigured, thus the finer body of Jesus; he therefore also saw and felt its wound when it was not the dense body of the flesh.

That is a quite natural happening which, supported by luminous helpers and forces for the purpose of convincing, was bound to make an all the more natural impression on Thomas, especially as it was willed by Jesus Himself.

But this very happening even supports quite clearly the fact that it cannot have been the gross material earthly body of Jesus, so familiar to all the disciples; for otherwise any doubt would have been out of the question from the beginning.

Therefore Jesus in His ethereal body *must* also have already had a *different* outward appearance, which admitted doubt of His genuineness through the difference from His otherwise well-known earthly body, so that Jesus still wished to give a special proof in order to remove the doubt which had become possible through the change.

Thus whatever such zealots wish to quote as grounds for their reasoning really bears within it a proof to the contrary! People must simply give up the rigidity of the indolent desire to cling to what they are accustomed to or what they have learned, then as they reflect upon it the illuminating ray comes spontaneously from all sides, so that later they can never understand why man has not thought of it much sooner.

And he who then summons up the strength to weigh one point calmly against the other will find that everything speaks for the *new* and nothing for the old, which has arisen from wrong, indolent thinking or clever calculation.

Surely earthmen constantly experience enough to be able with just a little reflection to think themselves easily into these facts. Who, for instance, has never yet experienced a clear dream in which the gross material body participates physically? It strikes out or weeps, sobs and screams, moans and speaks; whereas the dream, the actual experiencing, seeing and feeling, is by no means of a gross material nature, but much more delicate and fine than even the finer material substance, as was the case with the transfigured body of the Son of God during the incident with the doubting Thomas.

And yet, during his experience in the dream, man is completely convinced that it is of a gross material nature, and only on awakening does the recognition come to him that it was different, in spite of still finding gross material proofs in his tears and other things.

Also the so-called "transfiguration" is not the change of something that exists, such as the gross material physical body, but the uncovering of it, which allows a more delicate body to emerge, through which the human spirit itself can shine more strongly.

Indeed the transfiguration does not refer to the physical body either, but to man himself who is spirit, which after laying aside its physical body, and other clouding dross clinging to it, begins to shine ever more clearly through its coverings.

A new era is dawning which will remove all doubts, and allow the knowledge of God to arise anew in purer, more living raiment, which will not lessen the greatness of the Son of God's sacrifice at that time, but will place it in an even more radiant light, because the human spirit will have become knowing about it, and will not merely continue in a state of vague belief about it, a belief that bears no living power within.

# 88

QUESTION:

*As an earnest and thorough reader of all Abd-ru-shin's lectures, I am indignant at the nature of the article "Vomp and the Grail Settlement", which appeared in ..., because in the face of the true Word of Abd-ru-shin this can immediately be recognised as a masterpiece of deliberate distortion, intended to serve a definite but unspoken purpose.*

*Does Abd-ru-shin wish also to remain silent about this? And would it not be appropriate to give more detailed explanations about Mariolatry, because this must certainly also be of interest to non-Catholic Christians?*

ANSWER:

Why should I not continue to keep silent in answer to attacks which after all must be cleared up within a measurable space of time through the Divine Laws working automatically in Creation? The consequence will then be that just such attacks will not only fall back upon their originators, but more than anything else will contribute to advance the *opposite* of what was intended by them.

But since your questions are directly provoked by such attacks, I would like at least to give some hints which correspond to the facts, and which may encourage every human being to reflect and to think for himself.

Contrary to your opinion, the article you mention is

220

by no means a masterpiece of distortion, but the whole style is strongly reminiscent of the methods of the churches in the Middle Ages, which today are certainly universally condemned, with justifiable indignation.

The content and character of the article plainly show only *one* thing: the perhaps understandable anxiety, I will not exactly say fear, that many a deeper-thinking person, even from the ranks of the churches, might agree with the logical explanations about the Creation-Knowledge in my lectures, because they do not fail to give him an intelligible and convincing answer to all the hitherto unsolved problems of humanity, and relegate nothing to mysticism.

And with every word these lectures of mine are radiantly permeated solely with the purest, knowing veneration of God, emphasising His Perfection. Altogether, the Perfection of God is the basis and the starting-point of *all* my lectures, whereas with other teachings up to now this has often been disregarded; for Perfection permits of no arbitrary actions that lie outside the active Laws of Creation, since indeed the Laws of Creation have issued from the Perfection of God, the Creator.

This, however, exalts the worship of God and makes it even deeper in the knowledge; nor does it in the least belittle the sacred task of the earthly mother Mary of Nazareth, who was permitted to give the physical body to the Son of God Jesus!

And when, in acknowledging and emphasising the perfect Laws of God in Creation, I draw the conclusion that indeed according to the Laws of Creation earthly procreation is necessary for every earthly birth, there is

221

no defilement whatsoever in it; for otherwise every earthly motherhood would have to be regarded as a defilement! And will earthly humanity then presume to force God, in His automatically-working Natural Laws, to submit to their human, so diverse and also changing laws of society?

*Immaculate* conception is a conception in purest love, which is the opposite of a conception in sinful lust!

And it is self-evident that Jesus could *never* have been a child of sinful lust. I would be the first to oppose such a thought with the utmost vigour. It certainly needs a great uncleanness to interpret my purely objective observations in such a way.

With regard to your second question concerning the nature of Mariolatry, I will for once follow in the footsteps of the Son of God Jesus, and likewise elucidate it through a question:

Did Jesus, Who taught men *all things,* how they should think and act, indeed even how they should talk and pray in order to do what is right and pleasing to God, ever with even one word say anything of the kind? And Christians surely want to be guided by Christ.

I think there is nothing more to be said about this. Far be it from me to touch upon the convictions or views of other people, and I respect *every* worship of God if it is truly felt intuitively. Nor have I ever sought to force my knowledge upon anyone, but from the outset I always demand that each one should earnestly examine it for himself, because the personal responsibility invested in man by God also stipulates the possibility to make free decisions; for the Justice of God is also perfect; it would not hold man responsible for anything for which he could not make a free decision, which naturally makes no exception in matters of belief either.

And if in this case I were just to speak in the words of the Bible, on which of course many also rely, then according to the Gospel of Matthew, chapter 6, Jesus says:

"And when ye pray, use not vain repetitions, as the heathen do; for they think that they shall be heard for their much speaking. After *this* manner therefore pray ye."

Then He gave them the Lord's Prayer as it is still taught and prayed today. *But nothing else!*

And when I also point to the First *Commandment,* which Jesus also particularly emphasises more than once, and which explicitly states: "*I* am the Lord thy God, thou shalt have none *other* gods but Me!", this also demands a devout worship of God. All else is then thought out by men. And surely Christians only want to strive after *Christ.*

Already many years ago, however, I have also clearly explained in reply to questions that it is by no means wrong, and indeed even fitting, to thank spiritual helpers for their great assistance.

Let this be enough for today. He who has no unclean thoughts will never be able to find anything unclean in what I have said, but only objective reasoning in accordance with the Laws of Creation, which are based on the Perfection of God, as in most cases world history already demonstrably teaches.

World history! Indeed this too teaches many things besides, among others also that it has *always* been just the priests above all, irrespective of their conceptions of

God and their teachings, who acted in a wicked way against *every* Truth-Bringer and against those who sought the right conception of God, because they felt their peace and their influence to be threatened thereby.

Thus it was also the priests who oppressed the proclaimer John the Baptist and later the disciples, and who, led by the High Priest, accused the Son of God Jesus of blasphemy and brought Him to the cross.

And again it will be *world history* which, even in thousands of years to come, will also report with ruthless clarity the *facts* of the present time, and describe the struggles now taking place always in the same way, until the Truth of the Holy Light also shines through the most secret haunts of the Darkness.

# 89

QUESTION:

*I have read the booklet: "The World Teacher as Leader of Science" by Dr. Kurt Illig of Berlin, who writes as a Natural Scientist. Science surely also includes medicine. I have not yet, however, found anything in this field in the Grail Message. But a leader of science should, through hints and guidelines, definitely support any endeavours also in this field, which is so important to the well-being of men. Especially, for instance, in cancer research! Why is this not done?*

ANSWER:

Because the time for that has not yet come; for the leaders of mankind, and men themselves, are far more occupied at present with everything other than a healthy upbuilding. There can be no question of leading people out of this disastrous confusion in *all* fields, in view of the boundless conceit of knowledge which nevertheless still exists on the part of those who know nothing. And this conceit must absolutely fall to pieces through itself first, so that at last the lack of knowledge is admitted. Only after the complete breakdown of knowledge will ascent follow. These things are too valuable to be allowed to be cast into the present-day witches' cauldron of mutual self-adulation, where they would probably be ignored out of sheer vanity.

And the hour has already arrived when men must *no longer* be run after helpfully, as has hitherto been mistakenly considered Christian or humane. Men cannot take such love. It has only pampered them, and brought about an unhealthy over-estimation of themselves. Instead they will now be compelled at last to learn, through the most bitter experiencing, to distinguish between tinsel and real gold, so that all will not be completely lost.

However, since the above question is somewhat ironical, by way of an exception a hint shall be given, which will be referred to some time later to be dealt with in more detail: *Any cancerous growth is conditioned by the incapacity and insufficient activity of the liver!* This must be borne in mind. A healthy liver with a really normal activity does not allow any kind of cancer to develop. Therefore a correspondingly sensible way of living should already be strictly observed even with young people. And among those already ill, the emphasis should be placed mainly on that! With the recovery of the liver the power of the illness is broken, no matter where it is located.

# FINAL DECLARATION

I am absolutely indifferent to what people say about my Message and my answers to questions. Indifferent as to whether they like them or not. I am just as little moved by the warmest acknowledgements as by well-meaning letters of advice or even embittered attacks, whether they be of a decent or a contemptible nature. I know that for many human spirits the hour is no longer far distant when, from anguish of soul, they will forcibly break through the limitation of their inability to comprehend. *Only by this means* will they then learn to understand and to comprehend my words, which they must do if they do not want to perish in their present entanglement.

I go my way, untouched by friendship or hatred. Therefore I do not understand all the excitement of individuals and of whole groups; for whoever does not want my Word has only to leave It alone! After all, I do not force It on anyone, nor have I any intention of making a "business" of It. Let each one see for himself what he can make of It.

*Abd-ru-shin*

# INDEX

Psalm 22 4-5

"Our ancestors trusted you, and they put
were not disappointed."

**GRAIL PUBLICATIONS**

◊ ◊ ◊

P.O. Box 3568, Chénéville, Qc. J0V 1E0
Tel / Fax: 1 (800) 672-2898